"Joan Burbick and I (and a million others) live in a real and mythical place called The West . . . Rodeo queens are just as important to the idea of The West as Indian chiefs and gunfighters, but more important as their story has not been told. These women with epic hats, epic hair, and epic eye shadow tell epic stories."

—Sherman Alexie, author of
Indian Killer and *Smoke Signals: A Screenplay*

"[Burbick] succeeds in articulating [the rodeo queens'] ambitions and their anxieties, as well as her own insights, and she is capable of showing us both the glitter and the glamour of the rodeo subculture and, at the same time, some of its deepest contradictions."

—*Los Angeles Times*

"[Burbick's] intriguing book shows how changes in the role of rodeo queen have reflected changes in . . . the American West."

—*Dallas Morning News*

"Burbick brings a neglected part of Western Americana back to life in this delightful book of female rodeo participants. From contestants to queens, these remarkable women and their life stories are exciting and heartwarming. Even the topic of gender and racial bias is covered realistically. America's rodeo women are tailored with raw grit. A true treasure."

—*True West*

"A unique vein of regional history . . . [Burbick] turns a stereotype into individuals and portrays them sympathetically, avoiding feminist cant. The result is fresh."

—*Seattle Times*

"More interesting than the recollections of what it meant to be rodeo royalty is the historical framework—political, economic, social and cultural that Burbick builds around the women's stories."

—*The Oregonian*

"[Burbick] crafts an intriguing study of Western rodeo queens . . . profiling their lives in the spotlight and afterward."

—*Seattle Post-Intelligencer*

"[Burbick] combines a native's understanding of the territory with an outsider's skepticism. This is a writer and horsewoman who knows her subject."

—*Hartford Courant*

"*Rodeo Queens* is a thought-provoking and accessible book made even more attractive by the author's obvious fondness for her subject . . . a highly engaging book about a heretofore unexamined bit of Americana."

—*Bloomsbury Review*

"A wonderful souvenir of a rural and urban spectator sport . . . *Rodeo Queens* is an invaluable collection of memories from women who can still recall how the West was won."

—*Bookpage*

Rodeo Queens

ON THE CIRCUIT WITH

America's Cowgirls

Joan Burbick

PUBLICAFFAIRS

New York

Book design by Jane Raese

Library of Congress Cataloging-in-Publication Data
Burbick, Joan.
Rodeo queens: on the circuit with America's cowgirls / Joan Burbick.
(originally published as Rodeo queens and the American dream)
p. cm.
Includes bibliographical references (p. 217) and index.
ISBN 1-58648-204-1 (pbk)
1. Women rodeo performers—United States—History.
2. Rodeos—United States—History. I. Title
GV1833.5 .B87 2002
791.8'4'0973—dc21
2002028721

2 4 6 8 10 9 7 5 3 1

To Claire,
who listens for the laughter of horses

Contents

As my beloved aunt spoke, I saw what a horse and rider could do

when they aligned themselves of the same mind,

and thirdly aligned themselves with the mind of the land.

—Joy Harjo, "The Power of Horses"

Breakout

Every September, my local Idaho paper reprints the photographs of every rodeo queen past and present from the Lewiston Roundup. I have to unfold the paper and spread it across my kitchen table to get the full effect of these portrait shots, over sixty-five in all.

The faces staring out at me beneath the cowboy hats look pretty, strong, and confident. The hairstyles run the gamut from the classy bobs of the 1940s to the endless, mandatory tendrils of the Farrah Fawcett 1970s, a style with staying power into the twenty-first century. The cowboy hats shift from short, simple, squared-off brims to tall crowns, large enough to support the glamour of vertical rhinestone tiaras. Even with a cursory glance, I notice that the classic Western looks of the 1940s and 1950s gave way gradually to a glittery show-biz style that has yet to run its course.

Since 1935, when the rodeo started in Lewiston, a young woman from the community has been chosen rodeo queen either through tryouts or nomination to promote the annual celebration and represent the roundup at parades, county fairs, and regional rodeos. She usually has two princesses to help her. Together they form the "rodeo royalty."

The row after row of portraits resting on my kitchen table struck me as a story waiting to be told. Who were these women who promoted the rodeo? Why did they get involved in the first place? Were they real riders and ropers or only pretty faces trying to sweet-talk their neighbors into splurging on more rodeo tickets? And what did they think about their experience now, perhaps sixty years after their reign?

At first, I thought of the queens as a mere curiosity. I wanted to know why each September with clockwork regularity my local newspaper transformed into a high-school yearbook dedicated to rodeo royalty. But stories have a way of taking us by surprise. As I started talking to rodeo queens in Lewiston and other areas, I quickly realized their memories and lives were forcing me to rethink the history and culture of the West. Each woman's season as rodeo queen gave her intense contact with both the popular myths and the everyday realities of life in the American West. Together, their stories brought me close to both the clichéd Hollywood version of the cowboy-and-Indian Wild West and to the real problems of living on Western lands and among its diverse peoples. Rodeo queens lived at a junction between the old myths of the West and the heartbreaking reality of ordinary life. The tension in their stories was often fierce, both upholding and resisting conventional roles for women in the "Western." What these women wanted to believe would often push against and even contradict how they lived.

In recent years, the rodeo queen image has been pumped with pure adrenaline. At the start of the rodeo show, the queens burst into the arena with the energy of Calamity Jane and the accuracy of Annie Oakley. Called the "bust-out" or "breakout," this daredevil ride shows off their horse skills and wakes up the crowd. They spin and swirl on a dime, galloping at full tilt, wide open, and then screech to a halt in a cloud of dust. Cowgirls—slick in candy-red chaps or turquoise buckskin—get the blood pumping for the rest of the show: cowboys riding twisting bulls and bucking horses. Known as "sweethearts of the rodeo" by die-hard rodeo fans and as "buckle bunnies" or "cowboy cheerleaders" by fed-up rodeo haters, the rodeo queens are staples of the show.

Those few adrenaline moments in the spotlight at the start of the rodeo are generally one of only two times the audience sees the queens during the rodeo. The queens also ride the perimeter of the rodeo arena with the U.S. flag held high, joining the Grand Entry of rodeo cowboys and cowgirls, trickriders, pickup men, and local rodeo luminaries before the rodeo events begin. Then they usually sit their way through the rest of the rodeo as spectators, though a chosen few might be allowed to haze the cattle during calf-roping events or distribute prizes at the end. Their visibility as flamboyant cowgirls is almost in reverse proportion to their invisibility during the rodeo. Most of their work is done well before the rodeo begins. They are promoters—traveling, talking, appearing on radio and TV shows, riding in parades, and visiting schools to generate ticket sales and community spirit.

During the last century, there has been increasing pressure on rodeo queens to represent a more frenzied, commercial rodeo. As in most sports in the United States, the professionalization of rodeo has brought corporate sponsorship. Just like baseball, football, or basketball, rodeos now rely heavily on these sponsorships as a major source of income. Dependent upon Coors beer, Coca-Cola, Dodge trucks and Western-wear companies, rodeos use their queens not just to whip up support for the cowboys but also to sell, sell, sell. Instead of the star-spangled banner, rodeo queens often wave pennants for Bud, Resistol, and Wrangler. I have heard them referred to by rodeo organizers as "corporate icons," starry-eyed, all-American ingenues of big business.

But rodeo has always been a business, whether that of the local Chamber of Commerce or of corporate America. Its history is tied to the boosterism of small towns in the rural West. And now, even as it tries to link itself to a pastoral, nostalgic, premodern America of ranch life, it courts the dollar sign. Rodeo is big business.

And it's pervasive. On average, there are two Professional Rodeo Cowboys Association (PRCA)-sanctioned rodeos each day in the United States, with countless amateur rodeos, college rodeos, junior rodeos, and Little Britches competitions crisscrossing the nation. "Cyberodeo" has even penetrated the Internet.

I never have to travel far from where I live in the interior Northwest to attend a rodeo. Generations of rodeo queens live in communities nearby. Most of the interviews for this book took place within a 200-mile radius of my home. This region has a distinct Western history. Even though Lewis and Clark passed through this area in 1805, most of the permanent settlements by Euro-Americans weren't established until after the Civil War. Pioneer families trace their first homesteads back to the 1870s, late in comparison to the coastal areas, where the gold rush and shipping routes brought thousands from the eastern United States to booming cities like San Francisco and Portland. Not long after the arrival of these late pioneers, rodeo started in Pendleton, Oregon, in 1910. Rodeo rode the wave of popularity of Wild West shows produced by a new breed of entrepreneurs such as Buffalo Bill Cody and the Oklahoma Territory Miller boys, Joe, Zack, and George. And rodeo seemed to suit a region that often turned its back on the coast and looked toward Montana and Wyoming for cultural sustenance.

Since 1910, rodeo has expanded in the interior Northwest. Today, the PRCA has carved up the United States into twelve regions, each with its own rodeo circuit. Each circuit has a name such as Turquoise, Wilderness, or First Frontier, except for the really big rodeo states, which are merely called Montana, Texas, or California. The circuit in my part of the Northwest is called Columbia River, and it includes Washington, Oregon, and Idaho north of the Salmon River.

If you wanted to, you could attend forty-three PRCA rodeos in the Northwest each year and watch dozens of rodeo queens at each event. The year-round rodeo season officially starts in November, ending the next November with the National Finals Rodeo in Las Vegas, where the Miss Rodeo America (MRA) pageant also takes place. For the average fan, the season starts when the weather warms up in May and ends in September. A real devotee could kick the season off with the Coulee City rodeo in north-central Washington in late May and finish at Oregon's Pendleton Round-Up in mid-September. Of course, there are also hundreds of amateur rodeos and non-PRCA rodeos at county fairs and small-town celebrations throughout the area, such as Asotin Days and the Palouse Empire County Fair. If you lived near me, you could spend your life attending rodeos.

The Pacific Northwest states are also home to dozens of Indian reservations, each with its own powwow circuit, which often piggybacks on regional rodeos. Indian encampments are set up close to rodeo grounds. Dance and drum competitions take place a few yards away from bull-riding and bucking-horse contests. Certain tribes also participate in an all-Indian rodeo circuit that often has an all-Indian rodeo queen and court. Sometimes a PRCA rodeo will include an honorary Indian princess on the rodeo queen court, selected by the local Indian community to represent the tribe. Before 1953, the rodeo queens of the Pendleton Round-Up were frequently Indian women. They were not honorary Indian princesses. They were the real thing—the queen.

Washington State University, where I teach in the American Studies program, is only a short drive from both the Nez Perce and Coeur D'Alene reservations. The history of rodeo in this region is fused with the political, legal, and cultural complexities of Indian-white relationships. Telling the stories of rodeo queens necessarily raises the history of settlement and conquest, ethnic conflict, racism, blindness, and greed.

I have not tried to keep myself or my understanding of regional history out of this story. If I did, I would just be another in the hordes of tourists on pilgrimage and eager cowboy wanna-bes wandering the West. Fortunately, I live in a place that is neither an escape nor a nostalgic refuge from the pressures of the modern world. My West has its problems. I cannot imagine it outside the grinding force of personal and collective history, the drama of family migration and displacement, the pain of boom-or-bust economies, and the wild dreams of a fresh chance and a new start. I live in a place both scarred by systemic violence and sustained by daily human effort. Scratch the surface, and layers of racial and ethnic injustice emerge next to an unbridled desire to build a home and nurture the land.

Stories implicate the teller and the told. They test our allegiance and loyalty. They often lie. And so I chose to retell the story of the American West through my conversations with rodeo queens, allowing them to voice what the West means to them. Through their stories, I took a fresh look at what keeps the West an essential part of who we are as Americans. I was able to question the queens' identification with what historians call the frontier myth and its saga of cowboys and pioneers. And I was able to question my own beliefs about the land and its changing cultures.

But questions, of course, are dangerous. Before I started contacting and interviewing rodeo queens, I never understood how passionately many people feel about rodeo in their communities.

How much they hate it and how much they love it. I never realized how political rodeo can be. To some people it stands for everything good and wholesome in America, and to others, everything corrupt and artificial. Some people use it as a platform for their values, while others see it as only a form of entertainment. Still others wish it would go away and die.

I never thought when I began this project that political rain would fall all over my rodeo parade. I had a hunch that rodeo queens would want to talk about their version of the West and how that West still broadcasts a frontier vision of America. I never dreamed how confrontational this discussion could become, especially among the younger queens I interviewed.

Conflicts over the role of women in rodeo surfaced fast. The rodeo is packaged for testosterone thrills and spills. The rough-stock events of bull and bronc riding are the domain of men. Timed events like calf roping, steer wrestling, and team roping see the occasional cowgirl, but women are mainly confined to barrel racing. For over sixty years, rodeo queens have watched these competitions from the sidelines, and they have tons to say about them. Through their stories, I found out how the frontier mythology of the Western male action hero still manages to thrive and how it affects these women's lives. Next to the cowboy heroics of bronc and bull riding, rodeo queens are asked to play out a cowgirl fantasy. What they think about their role and how it affects them tells much about how women have lived in the American West.

At one point during my interviews, I was told bluntly not to "Betty Friedan it," and I have wondered how the author of *The Feminine Mystique* could have ended up as a verb, and a cautionary one at that. I have also been scrutinized by paranoid rodeo organizers who suspected I was a covert animal-rights activist or another type of potential troublemaker. Others cautioned me not to dig too deeply into tribal conflicts with rodeo boards. And I was warned about being an "outsider," even though I have lived in the West—the rural West, for that matter—for over twenty-four years, having settled in the Palouse region of eastern Washington in the 1970s.

One thing I learned through the years of talking with rodeo royalty was not to second-guess their lives or their stories. At times it was hard to listen. But listen was ultimately what I had to do. And not in some passive way like a tape recorder. I had to question, to prod, to tease out answers. And then I had to stop questioning and let their words rush out. Mainly, I would talk with women who agreed to talk with me—about forty rodeo queens from the 1930s to the present. We would go back and forth as I tried to follow a thread, or they tried to understand what I was about or what I wanted. Sometimes I had no idea where the interview was going and would wait to see which way the words drifted, maybe how a story about a horse butchered some fifty years ago became a parable of lost hope.

It would be accurate to say that their stories changed me. Some I embraced in sheer delight, others I resisted. The queens all made me think about how American culture produced a myth about the West that was so strong almost none of us can escape its grasp. Today, the West is a tenacious symbol of power and freedom, and the rodeo plays out that symbolism in ritual and sport. The winning of the West, its seizure from the hands of savages by spine-tingling action heroes, echoes throughout rodeo events. So does nostalgia for the ranch, the pioneer life, and the fantasy of the West as an escape from the boredom of civilized work and play. This cultural myth echoes each time a bronc rider wraps his hand around a plaited rope, raises his free hand to the sky, and jumps out of the chute on top of a ton of writhing horseflesh to the roar of the crowd. Rodeo cowboys and cowgirls perform this cultural play thousands of times a year in small towns and big cities. Their roles and images are recreated in movies and fiction, exported to Euro-Disney and plastered on Marlboro ads in the subways of Hong Kong.

This book starts down the rodeo road in the 1930s when queens witnessed the coming of rodeo to their small Western towns and ends with its transformation into Las Vegas glitter at the end of the century. Each queen's year as rodeo royalty is a touchstone against which to gauge changes in the West and in America. Their dreams, fears, and wry humor address the tensions between mythmaking and ordinary life. These queens rode the dust of the rodeo arena, watched the action, and left with a story to tell.

Rodeo Queen Lament

The locals called it the "smell of money." To me it lingered on the tongue, a mix of petrol and sauerkraut. Before I saw it, I tasted, then smelled it—a huge monolith of a paper mill on the Clearwater River, where it emptied into the Snake and headed toward the Columbia. At night, driving down the steep grade into Lewiston, Idaho, I could see the mill lit up below, an earthy constellation, thousands of electric lights illuminating the billows of smoke released from its clay-white vertical stacks. A ghost factory over a parched, harried land, the colossal timber mill dominated the town, operating with automated labor twenty-four hours a day. Computers worked its bowels, producing pulp for toilet paper, paper towels, and huge cylindrical paper rolls stamped for export to China and Japan.

Illegally built on Nez Perce lands over 100 ago as a trading post or "ragtown" for miners, Lewiston has seen gold digging, land rushes, and lumber mills shape its economy and culture. Never secure, its merchants and citizens have witnessed cycles of boom and despair. Extracting gold and trees has produced wealth for a few, but most locals live off a weakening service economy of minimum-wage jobs. Payday and title-loan businesses sprout up like weeds, offering relief to a town filled with the same consumer dreams as the rest of America but without the means to pay the bills.

When the first rodeo queen for the Lewiston Roundup was selected in 1935, the economy was worse. The papers were filled with labor violence, the tar-and-feather antics of vigilantes who did not take kindly to organizers, and disturbing news of soldiers shooting and killing people in places as far away and apart as Germany and China.

The year 1935 was a hard time to start anything. But in that year, a group of businessmen in Lewiston who were used to driving over to Oregon to watch the Pendleton Round-Up, one of the oldest rodeos in the United States, decided a rodeo was just what Lewiston needed. It might bring in money, help create community spirit, and at least give everybody in town a chance to play cowboy for a weekend or two.

The businessmen formed a rodeo committee, raised money, and started to organize the dozens of volunteers needed to put on a rodeo in a small town. The U.S. cavalry was stationed in Lewiston—it had been there since the mid-nineteenth century, when it kept in check (or exploited) the potential for violence in the social mix of settlers, miners, entrepreneurs, and Indian peoples—and their equestrian expertise was called upon in 1935 to help select the rodeo queen and her court. The woman eventually chosen rodeo queen had spent years working with horses that soldiers, not ranchers, rode.

"I didn't know that I was going to have to remember all that stuff," Dorothy protested. A solid, strong-faced woman with a head of thick white hair, she walked with a cane, but it didn't slow her down. I followed her into the kitchen, past her half-blind, deaf dog lying sentinel next to her husband, who watched TV from his

La-Z-Boy recliner. At eighty, Dorothy's clear voice and direct gaze woke me up. She was not going to bullshit about the past.

"A bunch of us girls used to ride at what they called a cavalry barn . . . A bunch of army guys, we rode their horses all the time. Regular army. This is way back. A cavalry unit just like the National Guard. There was a dozen of us girls who used to ride these cavalry horses on weekends. They had this one little horse, they called him Squirrel, a little sorrel. He had been a basic polo pony. And we used to ride in this big cavalry barn down there. And we would play tag and nobody could ever catch me. I was on this little polo pony, so quick. I was just holding on. We had these old McClellan army saddles with no horns on them, nothin' . . . They chose me out of twenty-one."

Dorothy saw her nomination for rodeo queen as another way to stay close to her beloved horses. One of the cavalry officers who helped to judge the queen competition recognized her gift and grit. Dorothy remembered clearly why she was chosen queen. "It wasn't my popularity and it wasn't my looks. It was my ability to handle a horse and ride. I was a horsewoman. Everybody used to come to our place. If they had a strange horse, I was on it before it got away from there. I'd get on anything."

Dorothy remembers being petrified of the social duties of the queen, meeting Chamber of Commerce members and speaking in public. After all, she was "just a country queen." Her princesses— the daughters of the downtown merchants and successful large ranch owners—came from a West she didn't know.

The portrait picture taken of Dorothy for rodeo publicity shows a young woman in an impossibly large cowboy hat with a scarf tied around her neck. "Oh yes," she said. They plopped that hat down on her head even though it was way too big and tied a scarf around her neck. They gave Dorothy her first pair of cowboy boots. Instant transformation: a rodeo queen.

Dorothy wasn't big on dressing up. As a young girl, she had worked on the family ranch wearing men's overalls and work shoes. In town she rode in jodhpurs and English-style cavalry boots. No one she knew had cowboy boots. Western wear was a novelty, a costume, like the rodeo queen outfit she was asked to wear. She still had hers, a buckskin skirt with black fringe, a fringed vest over a white blouse, a white hat, and black boots. A souvenir in mothballs.

Dorothy became the first queen of the Lewiston Roundup seven years after she and her brother had moved to the edge of town, where small-acre plots gave way to organized streets with names. Her family had been displaced from the land they loved, a ranch up on Eagle Creek near the Salmon River. Dorothy's brother and wife had run the Eagle Creek ranch until 1928, when they were forced to sell and then moved to town. Dorothy was about fourteen years old. That move was the continental divide in her life. Nothing was ever the same after that. She told me she can remember every detail about those years before the move to town; then life began to blur.

On the ranch, Dorothy got her first horse, a one-eyed Indian pony her brother gave her. "I used to ride that little old horse with one eye out in the point country when we used to bring the horses in to brand the colts and just run him down over these rocky hillsides. And he never fell with me, never ever fell with me. He'd turn his head sideways and just go."

"All I had to play with was horses," Dorothy says about her childhood, as she gazes at the backyard fruit trees she can no longer tend. We sit in her kitchen next to a table covered with bottles of pills. Her husband, who needs constant tending, is slumped in the next room, staring at the TV. Its static canned laughter spills over her words. "I used to break my own horses. It was just play. I was twelve, thirteen years old, you know. It was just play for me. I had this little bay mare, I called her Twilight and well, I'd just get on her, and she would buck me off, and I'd get back on again. Either she'd get tired or I'd outride her. One or the other. My brother's wife, she broke horses too. Well, her and I run the ranch. My brother he'd take off and go to the Forest Service and work up in the Forest Service and stuff. And her and I'd run the ranch by ourselves. We'd have to ride out the cattle every day . . . They sold out up there in 1928."

The 1920s sounded the death knell for many Western ranches. Conservative estimates claim that close to half of the ranches in states like Montana were foreclosed between 1921 and 1925. Bankruptcy was as common as huckleberry pie. The rural economic crisis sounded an early warning to the rest of the nation, but hardly anyone listened. A roller-coaster ride of wheat and cattle prices in the 1920s led to agricultural decline, and mining and lumber followed suit. The stock market crash of 1929 announced the depression for the rest of the nation.

Dorothy and her family sold the ranch and migrated to a rural Western town that had found a way to forget the failed dream of a prosperous, open West. For a precious weekend, Lewiston latched onto a publicity gimmick of rodeo hoopla, sprinkling the townsfolk with the seductive glamour of rodeo cowboys and trick riders. The rodeo would perform a story of individual adventure and endless possibility and reinvent the frontier past, bleached of poverty and loss. Maybe even boost spirits and get folks into the buying-local frame of mind—a jump-start for a groaning economy.

But Dorothy's rodeo had nothing to do with the economic dreams of her fellow townsmen. Her rodeo memories called forth a lament for loss irretrievable. Her summer as rodeo queen was a thin thread connecting her to a ranch world she had loved and lost. I had trouble coaxing her back to the 1935 Lewiston Roundup. Its importance had faded long ago. Now it was only a memory door to voice her yearning for the Salmon River country.

The longer we sat together in Dorothy's kitchen, the easier her ranch memories surfaced. Some came in a torrent. She remembered walking into the mountains and sitting for hours near the wild horse herds that grazed and watered near the Joseph Plains. The rapture was still in her voice after all these years, after marriage, raising children, and working in town as a bookkeeper. "I loved my horses, so crazy about horses. To this day I'd just give everything to have my horse. I don't know, I guess it was because up there on the ranch the only thing I had to play with were horses. I was up on the horses from the time I got up in the morning to the time I went to bed at night, I was out playing with the horses. I used to hike up in the mountains and be with the wild horses. Me and my old dog we'd hike up to the bluffs and go up in what they call the 'plains country.' And the wild horses they just ignored me as if I was one of them. I never thought about it. I just played like I was a horse."

She reached for her purse and took out a brittle, faded photograph of Pepper, her beloved horse, milk-fed, her "baby." Coal-black, long-legged, shiny, he nickered when she came. She trained him by herself, even taught him how to do a few tricks. "We raised him on a pan of milk. His mother rolled [died] when he was a little colt. I broke him. We brought him out to the Orchards when we came. I trotted him at thirty-five miles an hour behind a pickup. He never did shed, he just stayed shiny winter or summer."

"What happened to the ranch horses?" I asked. A bad question, one I immediately regretted. The horses? "Sold." Even the one the buyer had promised never to put down found its way to the rendering factory for dog food and glue. Except for a few saddle horses, every last one was sold. She would never forget the day they disappeared. The anger was still there, as if it had happened yesterday. "We had a hundred head of wild horses up in the Salmon River up there, what they call the 'high country.' When we left up there we turned them over to R. T. He sold them all for dog food. And my old saddle horse, twenty-one years old, she went along with them, too. I wouldn't speak to him for I don't know how long. We just brought out the four head, no, five head. My brother, he traded one for a milk cow. Holly, DoSay, Pepper, Traveler, and Spider."

I was not prepared for so much pain. I should have known better. In Dorothy's youth, horses fell like hail all over the West. Tractors were coming in fast, and it was not uncommon for a farmer or rancher to trade his entire working stock as partial down payment on the new machines. Horse culture throughout the West was taking a beating. Mechanization and foreclosures were not the only reasons for the slaughter. The horse herds of the Crow Indians in Montana and the Spokanes in Washington were shot en masse by the cavalry in the 1920s in order to undermine the Indians' stubborn resistance in holding onto the old tribal ways. Dorothy's first Indian pony and her magic wild horses could have been remnants of vast Indian herds. Her sadness exists within a web of loss.

Like the Euro-American, the horse was a relative newcomer to the western United States, that is, if you don't count the period over 10,000 years ago during the Ice Age when equids flourished in North America. By some accounts, the horse did not reach the Pacific Northwest until the eighteenth century, but when Lewis and Clark arrived in 1805, they were stunned by the massive herds raised by the Nez Perce living in what would become Washington, Idaho, and Oregon. The deep grasses, sheltered ravines, and canyons were a horse paradise, and the animals thrived, reproducing in staggering numbers and increasing the prosperity and mobility of the tribes. The Nez Perce also took quickly to cattle raising and would travel as far as California in the nineteenth century to find breeding stock. Their cattle and horse herds pitted them in a struggle over ranch land that was often violent and tragic. Land fraud, theft, and divisive treaties permeated the landscape. Non-reservation Palouse and Nez Perce faced eviction by railroad grants and hot-tempered farmers. Reservation Indians witnessed the boundaries of their homeland shrink with each new wave of miners and settlers. Access to water for cattle sparked fighting along the Palouse and Snake Rivers.

Dorothy's migration into town was another layer in the thick record of conflicts over Western lands and resources. "I cried when I left up there. I really missed it." The memory of Dorothy's ranch still haunted her. When she moved into town, she gravitated to the cavalry barn and a chance to ride. The rodeo was just another way for her to "be with her horse." But rodeo was a pale substitute for the open, free life of the ranch.

I have heard this same longing in the voices of other rodeo queens who lived in the Salmon and Clearwater River country in the 1930s and 1940s. They witnessed a beauty and experienced a freedom that now lives only in their memory. They felt privileged to have known the land as it was before the changes they see now, before the fast-food chains, the corporate sprawl of natural resource extraction, the federal and state land-use policies, the suburbanization of rural lands into ranchettes, the degradation of soil, water, and air. Locked in memory, the smell of sagebrush and pine, the clarity of the evening sky, the sound of horses running along a ridge haunts them in their old age.

Talking about the 1935 rodeo with Dorothy taught me that holding onto land was a central problem in the rural West. Almost no one inherits the family ranch. Maybe that is what the rodeo is saying: try to hold on, even for eight seconds, try if you can. Try to keep your connection to the land, to the wild. Try to run at breakneck speed around the arena without falling or losing your hat or your dignity. Just try. Keep getting up from the dirt, brush yourself off, and try again. Nothing can get you down. Gamble your body; you just might win. You just might remember the touch of the wild.

Dorothy's experience of rodeo had its roots in the society of cattle ranchers. Before the Chamber of Commerce turned rodeo into an organized, business celebration in Lewiston, informal rodeos brought together the white ranchers spread out in canyons, ridges, and plains around Eagle Creek.

Dorothy laughed as she described these impromptu gatherings. The cowboys would get a horse down and then try to saddle and ride the bucking bronc in a big pole corral. "They used to bring the horses in off the range, and they would just go crazy when they got them in the pen." Before the invention of the chute, getting the saddle on a horse was more difficult and dangerous than the ride. "That was really wild, really wild." The thrill of penning, downing, saddling, and mounting wild horses drew a fervent crowd. "People would ride for miles and miles and bring their food, pitch a tent, cook out in the open." These gatherings of ranchers would last up to a week and were times for distant neighbors to visit, play music, fall in love, and watch the crazy cowboys.

These ranch rodeos fed into the rodeo craze of small towns like Lewiston. Once in town, the rodeo was packaged by businessmen as a festive way to celebrate the American past, entertain the masses, and promote local stores. Well-established Wild West formulas easily blended with rodeo events. By the 1930s, the myth of the Wild West had been pounded into audiences through dime novels, stage plays, the booming film industry, and Wild West shows. Rodeo was merely the latest incarnation.

In particular, the Wild West shows set a pattern for rodeos. Since the mid-nineteenth century, these spectacles had been propagating images of Indians, cowboys, and cowgirls, creating a romanticized vision of frontier life in the American West. Twenty-three years before Dorothy was born, the World's Columbian Exposition of 1893, held in Chicago, glorified the frontier taking of lands. Buffalo Bill Cody's "Wild West"—he refused to call it a show—had its most profitable season in Chicago, with 6 million people attending. Cody's Wild West displayed lies, nostalgia, and adventure. The bloody, historical conflicts of the frontier were conveniently tucked into a fast-paced narrative of manifest destiny, pitting bloodthirsty, primitive Indians against brave, upstanding frontiersmen and cavalry, fighting for the valiant right to seize the land. These theatrical reproductions of the winning of the West were big business. They were also a cultural business, resolving the violence and conflict of conquest through the lens of entertainment.

Famous for his part in the Battle of the Little Bighorn at which General George Armstrong Custer died, Sitting Bull toured with Cody in 1885. He drew in big crowds that both applauded and hissed him. He smoked the peace pipe with Cody and rode in parades. His status as a shaman and warrior publicized the show, but he left after one season, sick of the noisy entertainment, the greed of white society, and the utter disregard for the poor he saw in the streets of American cities. In 1890, during the religious revival of the Ghost Dance among the Sioux, Sitting Bull was killed by Indian police sent to arrest him and bring him to James McLaughlin, the Indian agent. The events of Sitting Bull's death quickly became part of the show's publicity. Paul Reddin, the historian, describes how in 1893, the cabin where Sitting Bull was killed, complete with bullets, was set up at the entrance to the show in Chicago. Cody never missed a trick. Wars and conflicts with Indians made news. News was free publicity. Indians never won in Cody's world, but they were essential to bring in the crowds.

In 1893, masses of Americans knew about the frontier through popular pageants like Wild West shows, but the historical meaning of the frontier was only beginning to be explored by historians, anthropologists, archaeologists, and literary artists. While Buffalo Bill Cody's show played to throngs at the fair in Chicago, the Columbian Exposition also mounted ethnographic exhibits on the midway in Chicago. Replicas of Northwest Coast Indian villages, complete with performing villagers, entertained curious audiences with conflicting images of Indians as either progressive citizens or noble savages. Nearby, Frederick Jackson Turner gave his famous address to a group of professional historians, declaring that the frontier was the force behind the peaceful and progressive development of the United States. During the same period, Theodore Roosevelt and his friend, Owen Wister, author of *The Virginian*, promoted the cult of Anglo-Saxon masculinity by romancing the cowboy. The greatest story ever told, as the hucksters called it, the winning of the American West, had become a permanent part of American culture.

The heroic image of the rural West came just at the right time. In 1893, the United States was straining under urban immigration woes. Thousands of people from Southern and Eastern Europe tried to start a new life under the shadow of the Statue of Liberty. Thousands more African Americans traveled to northern cities, fleeing Jim Crow laws and economic hardship. The entire country witnessed a massive movement of people from the farms to towns and cities. Even in the rural West, places like San Francisco and Los Angeles beckoned white farmers trading in plows for city clothes.

In this time of social drift and confinement, the politics of race took a firm hold. "Separate but equal" became a euphemism for apartheid. The 2,000-mile border between Mexico and the United States rocked with violence over labor rights and land claims as revolutionary activities from Mexico spilled into the Southwest. On the West Coast, reactionary politicians introduced exclusion bills, and Congress prohibited immigration from China through a sequence of acts in the 1880s. Immigrants from Japan, India, and the Philippines were also refused entry during the first three decades of the twentieth century, and citizenship and land-ownership rights were restricted or denied to those already in the United States. Assimilation and its paranoid opposite, exclusion, shaped political debates, resulting in state and federal laws aimed at controlling alien elements in American society.

Out of this intense demographic change, the white, Anglo-Saxon cowboy and the red Indian emerged as convenient action heroes. These simplified stick figures propagated a frontier mythology that hid both the systemic violence of conquest and the modern incorporation of land and labor. Cowboy hats and warrior headdresses obscured the complex racial politics of the United States and created instead a romantic duel of white against red.

In Dorothy's memory of the Lewiston Roundup, the duel was barely alive. The only trace of Indian life in Dorothy's 1935 rodeo was the saddle she rode on. The saddle had belonged to Jackson Sundown, the Nez Perce championship rodeo cowboy. It is unclear how the saddle ended up in the parade and where it disappeared to afterward. I have heard the rumor that it now resides in a museum in Oregon. Dorothy wondered where it was, too: "I would like to know whatever happened to that saddle. All silver mounted. He won that at the Pendleton."

Sundown was a legend in the world of rodeo, having become a World Championship bronc rider at the Pendleton Round-Up when he was over fifty years old. In 1916, he had to ride three times before the judges would award him the title. The crowd cheered like crazy. Clearly the spectators were not going to let Sundown leave the arena until he was awarded what he had earned. He rodeoed in orange-and-black angora chaps, beaded and fringed gloves, and feathered hats with silk ribbons. He was considered one of the most daring rodeo cowboys ever.

Even though she grew up in the 1920s on traditional Nez Perce lands, Dorothy insisted that she knew no Indians at all, only stories about Sundown. No Nez Perce or any other Indians participated in the Lewiston Roundup when she was queen. Later, I learned from Gwen, one of Dorothy's princesses in 1935 and the daughter of the first president of the rodeo association in Lewiston, that Gwen's father, a successful businessman, had bought the saddle from Sundown. Aside from this fact, Indians were entirely absent from the 1935 rodeo in both Dorothy's and Gwen's memories.

It was not a coincidence that rodeo developed at the end of what some historians call the Indian frontier. By the 1930s, most tribal peoples were locked out of open lands and forced onto reservations. The year Sundown won at Pendleton was only thirty-nine years after the Nez Perce had fought and lost a bloody war with the U.S. cavalry, artillerymen, and infantry, sealing their confinement. Some accounts claim that during the war, Sundown fled with his family, escaping with two other young boys into Canada. Perhaps, Sundown resisted reservation life by rodeoing. The rodeo made him a hero to both white and Indian audiences. At a time when the winning of the West was ingrained as a national myth, Sundown twisted the plot and destroyed the facile opposition between cowboy and Indian. He stayed in the spotlight, refusing to vanish.

Now, however, only Sundown's saddle reminded Dorothy and rodeo fans that Indians had ever participated in the sport, let alone the town's history or present reality. In Lewiston, Indians had been reduced to unwanted players, hanging around downtown, pathetic and miserable. They had vanished into ragtag remains, leaving behind only white cowboys to compete for glory and white rodeo queens to ride triumphantly in the parade.

After I talked with Dorothy, I spent time reading the Lewiston paper and its coverage of the first rodeo in town in 1935. I was surprised to find out that Indians had not vanished from the public space but that their new roles were nothing Buffalo Bill Cody would have used for publicity. The year Dorothy rode on Jackson Sundown's saddle was also the year Archie Phinney, a local Nez Perce Indian, was lecturing at the Institute of History and Philosophy in Leningrad in the Soviet Union. Phinney had trained in anthropology with Franz Boas at Columbia University in New York and published *Nez Perce Texts,* an acclaimed ethnographic record of Nez Perce oral culture, in which his mother was the major Native American informant. Next to news of the rodeo in the *Lewiston Tribune* on September 29, 1935, were printed sections of a letter that Phinney had written to his mother. He reassured her that his research was going well and told her he had the daunting task of lecturing in Russian. The article ended with a tribute to his mother's skill as a traditional beadworker. She had recently completed a "bag with the American eagle" embroidered on its surface, using "the national colors." In these words, Phinney claimed his mother as both an American citizen and a traditional Indian.

During Dorothy's reign as rodeo queen, the newspaper also reported that a ten-piece Nez Perce jazz band entertained folks around the region. Now this really surprised me. A jazz band? I knew Lionel Hampton had been made an honorary member of the Nez Perce in the 1990s, but I had no inkling that jazz had been part of Nez Perce life for almost seventy years. How jarring these tidbits were to someone who had grown up on Westerns. Archie Phinney traveled to Russia representing the American West; a Nez Perce women designed beaded emblems, playing with the visual icons of dual cultures; and Nez Perce men played saxophone and trumpet to that new jazz beat.

But by 1935, middle-class white Americans had glutted on a diet of dime-novel Westerns and Wild West shows. Hollywood had been making a killing off Tom Mix–style movies, glorifying white cowboys. Scriptwriters and producers recycled chase scenes, replaying the same stories over again with increasing amounts of violence. Set against the open skies and vistas of the rural West, movie Westerns kept frontier formulas alive, and rodeos followed suit.

In 1935, the Lewiston Roundup rodeo committee wanted to cash in. Keep those horses running. Keep those cowboys bucking. Keep those dollars flowing. When that cowboy hat was plunked down on Dorothy's head, it didn't matter if it fit or not. It was there to stay. And stay it did.

When I left Dorothy's home, I asked her if she still went to rodeos in town. She replied that it was impossible to go because of her husband's illness and her housebound life. Nodding at her husband, who sat dozing in his recliner, she turned to me, smiled, and said, "We watch the rodeos on TV all the time."

I could not get Dorothy out of my mind when I woke up at the crack of dawn a few months later to watch the rodeo queens prepare for the Lewiston Roundup annual parade down Main Street. The parking lots at the west end of town were frantic with parents, horses, rodeo queens, and princesses. The groups were color coded. A cluster of robin's-egg-blue fringed leather chaps. A trio of metallic-silver Western shirts. A duo of pink-so-bright-it-hurts-your-eyes cowboy hats. Satin or leather sashes in coordinated colors, draped over horses, proudly announced each rodeo royalty's home: Walla Walla Frontier Days, Lewiston Roundup, Elgin Stampede, Chief Joseph Days, St. Paul Rodeo, the Snake River Stampede.

The queens hovered close to their princesses while their mothers scurried past, racing for last minute hairpins and buckskin gloves. Everyone was on high alert.

Most had been wide awake since before dawn, washing down their horses with bottles of Cowboy Shine, spraying on cans of horse glitter, and attaching armfuls of plastic flowers behind their saddles over the rumps of their parade horses. Each horse took hours of care, as did the women's hair. Curling irons were the new weapons of this Western pageant. Cascading curls under tiara-crowned cowboy hats ruled.

As the start of the rodeo parade neared, nervousness cut through the cool morning air. Parents nagged and cajoled. Seventeen-year-old rodeo queens barked back or practiced their smiles. I strained to snap some photos and carry on conversations with a few of the royalty before they climbed on their horses and joined the long line of marching bands, floats, and the team of Budweiser Clydesdales. The rodeo parade was a big event in this Idaho town. Even people who never went to the rodeo would come with collapsible plastic chairs, coolers, and kids to watch this show. Free candy and clowns magnetized the crowd.

I didn't talk with too many rodeo queens that morning. Their eyes quickly drifted off to their horses or their outfits, fresh from the dry cleaner, all under strict orders to stay spotless. Occasionally, a father who had found out that I was writing about rodeo queens would wander over and talk about how hard his daughter had worked, the hours she'd put in to train her horse, or the tears spent over finding the right mascara.

I noticed nearby a group of traditionally dressed Nez Perce preparing a float. After a period of anger, frustration, and conflict with several rodeo committees, the Nez Perce have begun to participate in the rodeo parade. Three women were spreading blankets and banners over the float's edges. They covered the blankets with beautiful beaded bags and woven baskets. Several eagles and American flags were woven into their designs. Like the beadwork of Archie Phinney's mother, the eagle reflects both traditional Indian and patriotic American associations, a motif playing with vivid red, white, and blue, perfect for graphic design, perfect for weaving together overlapping cultural worlds. No simple world of cowboy-and-Indian opposites, but a world of shifting borders and transformations. A world of exchange and perseverance.

Clicking off my tape recorder, I walked away from the whirlwind of parade preparation and settled into the simplicity of watching. I covered up my camera lens, found a soft square of grass, and let the noise of the bands warming up and the sounds of the fire trucks and floats lining up drown out the long list of questions buzzing in my mind. Nearby, the Clearwater and Snake Rivers rushed into blue-green confluence, then slowly drifted by the expectant scene. I sat back and thought about how Dorothy would have looked riding down Main Street on her borrowed horse and her borrowed saddle. I thought about her grief and the catastrophic change this community and its tribal neighbors had experienced in the last century.

I was flat amazed by the staying power of the rodeo.

The Last Branding

The land disappeared at Rattlesnake Grade. One minute, green ponderosa pines offered shelter. The next, the bottom fell out. Endless blue sky descended toward undulating bands of buttes, ridges, and canyons, meeting the land at a bowled horizon infinite miles away. Panorama was not an adequate word. The landscape swallowed travelers and hurled them to the canyon floor.

Even though I had driven Rattlesnake Grade dozens of times over the last twenty years, I still had a healthy fear of its curves, vertical spins, and scant guardrails. With only about nine miles to the canyon floor and the Grand Ronde River near the border of Washington and Oregon, the journey felt more like a mental fifty. The drive took me about forty-five minutes from rim to floor, and I was not the slowest one on the road, not by a long shot.

Once I made it to the cool shade and safety of the river bottom where willows and cottonwoods thrived, I drove west up the Grand Ronde toward Maxine's home, a cattle ranch stretched about a mile down both sides of the river canyon. Maxine was on the rodeo court one year after Dorothy in 1936, but unlike Dorothy, she never lost the ranch. Maxine married and raised a family in this canyon, and she intended to stay there until she died.

I had been invited to spring branding. It was to be Maxine's last. She and her husband, Ivan, were selling off their herd to a neighbor and retiring from the grinding work of raising cattle. They hoped to live on the ranch with the luxury of free time. Today the neighbor's brand would be seared into the hide of all the new calves. Not one of their three daughters had come to watch.

I had met Maxine, Ivan, and two of their daughters, Randa and Zana, at a bar in Lewiston a few weeks earlier. All three of the girls had been on rodeo courts in the region. We sat at a dark back table, drank beer, and told stories.

Maxine would have liked to be called flamboyant. She was dressed in a tailored-tight, pink-and-red Western suit and wore long beaded red earrings. Her husband sat near her listening to the banter of his family. Her daughter Randa announced right away that she had not married a cowboy and was living in Spokane. Zana, the quietest, sat back away from the table.

Restless and skinny, with a voice marked by a nervous laugh, Maxine darted her eyes across the table and told me she was "not too shy." Her family all grinned at the remark. She wasn't sure what I wanted, but she was ready to play. Her rodeo past she viewed with a sense of humor and farce. She sat at the edge of her chair and had a hard time keeping her hands still.

When Maxine was young, she was all cowgirl, and at eighty years old, she still liked to ride in rodeo parades. "I think I am kind of a flashy rider, but not the best at handling a horse. I mean I can handle a horse, but I think I am more of a flashy rider." Always at the edge of control, Maxine was no sissy rider who kept her horse tight and under hand. She rode like she talked, and her words were as brash as her clothes. Red and hot pink. She loved every minute of her year as rodeo princess. "I love to see people. I like that. I am just a little country gal. Boy, I was really living high." Her husband sat back in his chair and smiled; both daughters shook their heads. Then they asked her to tell the story.

At first, Maxine hesitated. She couldn't believe they wanted her to tell that story, especially to me. But with everyone's encouragement, she dove right in and had to fight hard not to laugh her way through the telling. It was back at the 1936 rodeo that Maxine was forced to ride a "green-broke old horse," a horse barely used to having a person on his back. Her own horse, Dixie, had fallen and broken a kneecap five days before the rodeo. Maxine's brother Russ had come to the rescue with Raleigh, too much horse with too much head.

Raleigh was a handful. Russ had thrown him in the rodeo arena and wrestled him to the ground. It was like old-time ranch rodeo. No chutes. Just the thrill of getting a horse down and waiting to see what would happen when somebody fool enough would try to ride him up. In 1936, plenty of people hung around to watch.

Maxine made sure I understood the drama. "Every time you get a horse down you get a big crowd—Casey Tibbs, Bud Linderman, big cowboys, you know, and here I am really getting excited because we are gettin' all this attention." Maxine was there as a rodeo princess whose main job was to promote the rodeo, but maybe, just maybe, she would get her chance to work a bucking horse before the best rodeo cowboys.

Almost out of her chair, Maxine waved us all into her story. "So this old horse they got him thrown, and I think it kind of got to this old horse, you know, to go through all this. But anyway, he kind of got up, his front feet with his hind end sitting down—horses can do that, you know. But anyway my brother was kind of a character. And he says, 'Okay, Max. Get on him and whip him where the colt sucks.' So I like a dumbbell got on that old horse sitting half up, ya know, and I was scrunched down on the saddle. So I took a short rein with my left hand, pulled my hat down because you don't dare lose your hat, and then I got a death grip on my saddle horn. I said, 'Okay, Russ, turn him lose.' That old horse got up. He let loose a few unseemly noises, and staggered off down the row. I could have shot him. Here I am ready to show off."

Maxine was ready to buck that old horse out. But Raleigh had less glorious ambitions. All he did was stand there and fart. Sitting in the back of the dark bar, Maxine howled with laughter at the memory, and her family joined the joke. The raucous energy turned heads at nearby tables. She had tried to play bronc rider for world-champion rodeo cowboys and left the rodeo arena without prize money, but at least she had a good tale. It was all about fun.

The longer I sat in the bar with Maxine and her family, the more clearly I saw that rodeo was an escape from their hard life on the ranch. They had no vacations, but nearby rodeos gave them three weekends off a year. And if you were rodeo royalty, even better—you had permission to play. In 1936, Maxine's duties were brief and local—a few parades, public appearances, and, of course, the grand entry at the rodeo itself. Her daughters had more responsibilities, but I doubt as much fun as Maxine. She also fell in love at the rodeo. Ivan had watched her tryout for the queen competition on her horse, Popcorn. His voice still shines with admiration for her daredevil ways. After the rodeo, Maxine and Ivan were married and started raising their family.

The rodeo gave Maxine the chance to be treated "like a queen," an honor that continues up to the present. Maxine reminded me, "If you are ever in the Lewiston Roundup, you are there forever. They treat me more like a queen than anything right now. I am the oldest that can still ride." And ride she does, every year in the annual rodeo parade. She balks at the term *lady* as a description for a

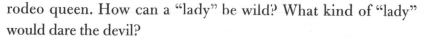

rodeo queen. How can a "lady" be wild? What kind of "lady" would dare the devil?

I replayed the conversations of that night out with Maxine and her family as I drove to the spring branding. I smiled at the memory of a red and hot-pink Maxine, laughing loud and long. When I finally arrived at her ranch on the Grand Ronde and walked into her kitchen, I saw right away that Maxine was in a different mood. She did not have much time to talk. Her stories in the bar had disappeared. She was rushing to get food together for family and friends who had been working with the cattle since dawn. She was focused, intense, and not about to interrupt her pace with my questions about rodeo queens. I offered to help but was told everything was okay.

I was to learn more about Maxine from her neighbors that day. Maxine was "raised out back Anatone," a tiny town a few miles north of Rattlesnake Grade, and "always had cattle." Ivan grew up near the Grand Ronde and knew the river canyon ways and what type of cattle could best graze its steep hillsides. Together they had held onto their cattle ranch through good times and bad. Today was the end of an era for the entire family. The daughters were not here to see the switch. They could not bear it. I was surprised Maxine and Ivan let me come by at such a time with my tape recorder, camera, and questions, especially as Randa had warned me ahead of time not to mention the change out loud.

Despite the sober situation, laughter filled the house as Maxine ran around setting out dishes of macaroni salad and beans on the dining-room table. Outside, a dozen yards from the back door, two men and a woman ran a calf through a narrow corral to a metal set of holding braces and a squeeze chute that flipped the calf on its side. It was quickly vaccinated, branded, and, if necessary, dehorned and castrated. The whole procedure took only a few minutes for each calf, leaving it dazed and ready to run.

Randa, Maxine's youngest daughter, had talked with me on the phone before I came about what was going to happen. She wanted to reassure me that the calves were not harmed, but that some people are disturbed by all the noise they make, their struggles to get out of the holding bars, and the snot, blood, and saliva flying about. I tried to reassure her that I could take it, having seen many injuries at horse barns over the years—barbed-wire gashes, puncture wounds, and horses ballooning with colic.

I wandered outside and noticed Ivan leaning against a fence rail, watching his herd being renamed. The hot iron of the brand changed the legal owner of each cow and steer. Ivan waited stoically by the corral and said nothing. The pile of horns and discarded needles grew taller next to the squeeze chute. He offered to let me ride one of his cow ponies down the road if I wanted something to do. I thanked him and left him alone with his thoughts.

Later that afternoon in the living room, I heard about how Ivan had tried once before to retire. He even tried fishing to make the transition easier. The Grand Ronde runs right through the ranch, and fisherman from all over the United States come to float its current and try their luck at catching steelhead. Ivan tried, too. He rode his horse down to the riverbank and cast his line without getting down from the saddle. But he didn't see much point to it, and he was back buying and working cows within months. Maxine echoed his rejection of recreation. She laughed and said that by ranching, they "didn't have to jog." Recreational punishment belongs to urban dwellers who tumble by like leaves in a storm. They just pass through; they do not belong.

Staying on the land has not been easy for this family. Maxine insisted that there was "something satisfying about owning land," but the future of the family ranch was unclear. Even though Maxine and Ivan's three daughters have all been on rodeo courts, not one is a ranch woman. The oldest daughter, Zana, has a son who was working hard branding the cattle today, but he normally works a full-time cowboy job down the river. I talked with him only a few moments during his quick lunch. He was in a hurry, and what he did say made work the message. "I get only a couple days off a year." No weekends, no holidays, no paid vacations. No sick leave, no mental-health days, no personal days. He reminded me that cattle never take time off. His grandfather was up at four that morning getting the cattle fed and ready to go.

Despite the chosen work of the grandson, there was a generational divide in this family. While Maxine and Ivan held tenaciously onto the ranch, their daughters spoke of it with nostalgia and yearning. The youngest, Randa, tried to explain to me what all these changes meant to her and her sisters.

All three daughters worked the ranch growing up, driving cattle and doing what was needed to keep the family business going. They knew hard, physical labor from morning until night. Now their ranch work was confined to weekends and certain times of the year when they helped out with their husbands and children. Cut off from the daily routine of ranching, Randa felt an urge to pass on the "essence" of the cowboy to her children. She was clear about it: "I always take my fifteen-year-old son back to get as much of it in him as I can. So whenever I can go back when we ride with the cattle, bring them down, or take them up to pasture, I take him." To Randa, the ranch represented not a place to live but an attitude toward life. "It's being who you are all the time. It's not worrying about those little things. It's all those basic, human cowboy principles that the true cowboys have. About doing unto others and hard work. Never giving up. Never giving up."

More than anyone in the family, Randa wanted me to understand the debt she felt toward her parents, especially her father. "He taught us everything we know. He was always there teaching us and encouraging us, a real hands-on. Directions, you know, how to learn to get back if you get lost. Killing a rattlesnake when you see it, shut the gate for your neighbor, and fix the fence if it needs it. The whole learning thing, like one-on-one."

But Randa didn't marry a cowboy; she lives hours away in Spokane without any chance or desire to return to ranching twenty-four hours a day. She can only imitate those moments of working right next to her parents. "Like I took [my son] on a paper route. And I got right out there and did it with him. It was hard but I thought, you know, it's what Dad did with me. We're together. Sleepy together, cold and wet and tired together, but we were still together and doing it." What she practiced daily on the ranch as a child had become a set of ethical guidelines for her children who do not live on a ranch and probably never will. I wondered how they make sense of these rules severed from the taste and smell of necessity.

Cut off from the ranch, Randa gave more meaning to the rodeo than her parents did. For Maxine, the rodeo was merely an escape from hard ranch labor. It was a scene of farce and romance. For Randa, the rodeo symbolically connected her and her children to the ranch. It had become a substitute for the ranching life and a way to keep in touch with what she called Western values: hard work, perseverance, community.

The rodeo meant something different for everyone in this family. Maxine relished the memory of her past daredevil self who rode horses without fear. Ivan, the time when he fell in love. Their daughters, who lived away from the ranch, used the rodeo to hold onto a belief in the "cowboy" way of life. They were left to remember their old lives as they faced a new world without fences, barbed wire, cows, or open sky.

During lunch break I wanted to talk rodeo, but they wanted to talk cattle. I sat in the living room, balancing on my lap a plate piled high with baked beans, green salad, and a hamburger. I listened to the neighbors gossip about ranchers who lived up and down the river canyon. There were few secrets here. How fellow ranchers cared for their animals made for hot conversation. A story emerged about one neighbor whose unexplained anger had exploded; he chained his dog to the back of his pickup and drove into town, killing the dog. The man's cruelty did not go unnoticed. In these parts, if you did not take care of your animals, you were as good as dirt.

These ranchers were talking about ethics and politics, and they wanted me to join in. Chitchat about rodeo could wait. They were all bothered by the lack of knowledge "out there," meaning, I think, in my world. These ranchers felt frustrated and alone. Who was listening in America? They felt the media, more than helping, muddled the issue. For the last twenty years, the ranch had become a battleground. For them, the war on the West started during the 1980s, when environmentalists took on the ranchers, accusing them of overgrazing both public and private lands and polluting the waterways.

In reaction, federal and state laws restricted grazing rights on public lands, sinking ranches further into debt and indecision. The most radical environmentalists wanted ranches shut down. They warned about the erosion of the land and the degradation of streams. Cattle had to go, period. In response, some ranchers were fighting for what they saw as their very existence. They believed they would be displaced from the land. Since the 1980s, the rhetoric has toned down somewhat, with more attempts to negotiate solutions on how to preserve Western lands and still have cattle ranching remain viable. But the sense of threat was still thick, and solutions have been difficult to find and enforce.

Ivan and Maxine were not in the room when these hot topics came spilling out. Ivan was still outside by the corrals and Maxine was in the kitchen. The two seemed to work right through the controversy. It was as if talk was cheap and only hard work could keep the land in your family. Just keep working.

Maybe I could write about the conflicts, a neighbor suggested. I stared down at the thick hamburger that I had just plopped on my plate and thought about the food I was about to eat. Over stretches in my life, I have been a vegetarian but even then realized my shoes and handbag came from those four-footed creatures I wanted to protect. I have used by-products of the cattle industry, often without realizing it: the enzymes, blood extracts, and other by-products that filter through the food chain; the pharmaceutical and cosmetic products; and countless solvents necessary for industrial production. Was I really aware of all that cattle offered up on the altar of my culture? Probably not.

Today the lands that rise up out of the Grand Ronde river canyon forming the Umatilla National Forest contain huge tracts used by ranchers through a network of grazing rights. Federal and state land-use policies dictate the movement of cattle and horses on every square inch of soil, creating a labyrinth of bureaucratic forms, court orders, rules, public hearings, and revisions. Resentments are high even when the goals are mutual—to sustain and preserve the land.

But environmentalists and government regulations are not the only problems for these ranchers. The fast-food industry and the corporate structure of meatpacking have brought cattle ranching to its knees. As Eric Schlosser wrote in his book *Fast Food Nation*, four giant meatpacking firms slaughter 84 percent of the cattle brought to market. Family ranchers have little leverage on issues of quality or pricing. Like poultry farmers, they have been reduced to the lowest level of supplier. Pressed up against the demands of

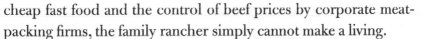
cheap fast food and the control of beef prices by corporate meat-packing firms, the family rancher simply cannot make a living.

I thought about another rancher a few months earlier who told me that it made him sick what was being fed to cattle today. Cheap feed was essential because the price of beef kept plummeting. As a result, the beef in the grocery store had no taste, and no one seemed to care. Worse, fast-food hamburgers disguised a multitude of sins. It was amazing what evils mayonnaise—what some people called white slime—could mask. Maybe mayonnaise was how we got through the day. Smear on enough and you never had to know what you were eating or how you were living or what difference knowing would make.

As I sat staring glumly at my hamburger, I realized how much anxiety pulled against the easy banter of the conversation in the living room. Squeezed between the demands of the market and the anger of environmentalists, some ranchers saw threat everywhere. To make it worse, in 1992 for the first time Americans ate more chicken than beef, and since then the safety of beef has been hammered by cases of *E. coli* and mad cow disease. The fact that ranchers think of themselves as victims is not surprising.

I bit into my hamburger, looked out at the cattle that grazed the hillside, and listened to the voices of these men and women who depended upon those grazing animals outside for their livelihood. Family pictures of two generations of rodeo queens dotted Maxine's living-room walls. Their smiles offered reassurance and lent a warm happiness to the room. They consoled, but they were also a consolation prize for the daughters not on the ranch. I could not resist how good the hamburger tasted. Outside the window, a nodding cow caught the sounds from the living room and glanced my way, expectant.

Some who write about the West have argued that we need to save the ranch because it is our tradition. Cowboys tending cattle on the open range is an indelible part of our collective past. But it all depends upon how we count time. The richness of this land has been known for hundreds of years. In the nineteenth century, the Grand Ronde valley was a refuge for the Nez Perce, who would drive their large horse herds into its protective walls during the winter months. Later, when cattle came their way, the Native Americans brought them into this haven. White ranchers were late arrivals, some moving here after they had grazed out lands further south in Oregon. Their inability to sustain an economic world left them restless and acquisitive. The rich, warm land of this canyon was a new Eden and a second chance. They drove the Nez Perce out of the lush river valley.

Many early homesteads in this part of the West first raised sheep and tried their hand at dairy farms. Immigrants coming into the United States in the early twentieth century had a hunger for food from the "old country," where lamb and mutton were common fare. Their children's tastes changed. In the 1930s and 1940s, cattle barons used rodeo to promote beef, and today some rodeos still have a clear link to stockmen's associations. After World War II, Americans hungrily embraced the chain hamburger stands that spread across the United States. The postwar years witnessed a big boom for rodeo and beef consumption, though the beef boom is abating today in this more heart-conscious, aging society.

While millions of Americans gobbled up beef, very few were willing to live a life revolving around cattle. Long ago in the nineteenth century, people understood that cattle work produced nothing but low social status and dead-end lives. Some might want to play cowboy as a right of passage to "manhood" or as a break from the routine of work, but few would rise at 4 A.M. to give an animal food, see a cow through a problem birth, or tend a horse's wounds. As one rodeo queen from the 1940s who came from a successful ranch family put it, "I don't want my sons to be ranchers."

The land had become a prison, a tightening vise. It caused heartache and heartbreak, worry and isolation. What, I wondered, would make someone stick it out on the ranch? No wonder Randa and Zana refused to live this life twenty-four hours a day.

The branding was finished, the meal was over, and the dirty dishes were piled up in the sink. I stayed around and helped as much as Maxine would let me. Later that afternoon, driving home back up the grade, I thought about cattle, not rodeo. The horses I saw today were trained to work with cattle. The dogs were trained to work with cattle. The people were trained to work with cattle. Everything revolved around cattle. Acres of land were planted with hay and harvested to help feed the herds during the winter months. Tons more had to be bought and hauled in. The grade was steep and winding, the soil dry and etched with fissures and ravines.

Critics of the cattle industry point to this waste of land and human resources to produce a form of food easily replaced by more environmentally friendly crops such as soybeans or lentils. In contrast, ranchers often see themselves as guardians of the land, helping the elk and deer herds that wander across their property, searching for food.

Maxine and Ivan made a choice even though they were faced with an uncertain future. Having land brought them peace of mind, and even what Ivan called "health." The sound of the river was a constant in their daily lives. The steep angle of the terrain upstream was the scene of stories from their childhood. To them, the landscape of the Grand Ronde was a history of families who had come and gone. Most of the small ranchers and the one-room schoolhouses dotting the river canyon had disappeared. Ivan and Maxine sensed absence where I saw only empty space. But they would stay even if their children would not.

The day had been long. As my car worked hard to get to the top of Rattlesnake Grade, I let the tape recorder in the seat next to me run on while I remembered another interview with a 1946 rodeo queen, Barbara, who also grew up in this same harsh cattle country. Her father had worked for years with sheep to gather enough money for a down payment on a ranch not too far away on Joseph Creek.

Barbara could hardly stand to watch Westerns like *Lonesome Dove* on television because they were "so untrue." She wondered how the rodeo she knew could have been turned into a Hollywood make-believe world. Women dolled up and rode around on horses covered with glitter and plastic flowers. They wore plastic smiles and waved like mechanical toys at a celebration hardly anyone understood. Gone were the flies, the sickness, the brush, the wire gates, and the pain. Gone were the few rare gentlemen who respected the rights of Indians. All that was left were cowboys with an attitude and without cows. Barbara warned her children against becoming ranchers, but she confessed that ranch land could not be so easily left behind. She had to return periodically to her brother's ranch to listen to the coyotes and lean in the wind.

The top of the rim caught me in pine trees again. I welcomed the coolness and the protection of the ponderosas and Douglas firs. I remembered how as a child this smell of pine marked a boundary between my Chicago brick winters and my summer days in the Rocky Mountain West. The earth plunged into sky-shapes more majestic than scrapers. Magpies jumped on the side of the road; their long stiff tails, flicking up quickly, balanced their agile bodies as they scavenged for food. On the long three-day drive from Chicago to Colorado, my sisters and brothers used to play a game to see who could first spot a magpie. The magpie meant we were almost there. Its geometric slash of white and hidden band of dark turquoise brought us to the border of open country, a wild space, alert and listening.

How we own this land will determine how we belong to it. Its beauty and hardness have tempted too many into greed, stubborn resistance, and defensive politics. Once I saw a lone cow perched up on a ridge in a canyon with steep rocky walls. Afraid to back up, it stood there, gripped by fear. The cow saw no choice but to stand there frozen and die. But choices are often a matter of perception. The anxiety of ranching can freeze people. The way out requires forbearance, flexibility, and collective determination.

Many families on the Grand Ronde have left for cities and towns. Some like Randa find a provisional way to hold on—the occasional weekend on the ranch or the rodeo parade. Others like Barbara bolt outright, stung by the pain. Maxine and Ivan hold on, hoping for the best but knowing the generational continuity is gone. Rodeo continues, but not the ranch.

3

A Drowned Land

Darkness gave way to a small but brilliant sunrise hanging on the horizon, the glow of a cheap bauble from a small-town dime store. Too orange and too red. Birds kept showing up on the road. Crows in groups of three or four darted across the highway, flying low. I was invading their turf. The night highway was their grocery store, free roadkill provided by unsuspecting drivers, a scavenger's food park.

In the dawn light, a massive red-tailed hawk landed on a stark yellow road sign, its wings waving me past. Ahead, the highway flattened out into the scablands of central Washington, named as if this landscape were human skin, stretched out and wounded, thick with scars. The sculptured wheat fields gave way to boundary rock edges and streams digging into soil, carving gullies and small canyons, creating havoc with the geometry of wheat. Bunchgrass, Indian parsnip, and blue-green clusters of sagebrush hugged the ground, trusting the thin topsoil against steady wind. The town of Dusty faded in my rearview mirror.

I was to meet JoAnne at the phone booth on Highway 26. Everyone in this part of the state knows where it is. She knew that I would know where it is, even though it's about seventy miles from my home. When I pulled off the road, JoAnne was sitting in a beat-up red pickup complete with horse trailer. Stepping out of the large truck, she looked small and fragile. I would later discover my eyes had deceived me. JoAnne was as strong and lightning quick as the cow horses she handled. Wiry and friendly, her long black braid swung around as she held out her hand to mine. She was in a let's-get-going mood, and I followed her in my car, driving north toward her friend's ranch. JoAnne had told me she did not like to drive in town, and I wondered what that meant as I tried to keep up with her pickup as it sped down the highway and turned fast onto a maze of gravel roads.

Twenty minutes of hard driving later, I was sitting in her friend Marie's kitchen, admiring her collection of salt and pepper shakers. Marie's husband, Les, showed up and dug through some drawers in the kitchen, awkwardly trying to bandage up his hand. An old wound from barbed wire had started bleeding again.

While Les and JoAnne talked about getting the horses ready, Marie asked me to sit down and with pride told me JoAnne could herd cattle like a man. JoAnne was even asked by local ranchers to locate errant cows hidden in gullies and ravines. She was the genuine item, a cowgirl who knew how cows behaved and had a horse trained to do the job of catching them. In the dark kitchen, Marie confided that no one knew anything about ranching anymore. She and Les had picked up a steer and parked it down by the city sports field in Lewiston once, and some kids had come over to see what was in their truck. She had told them it was a steer, but they probably hadn't even understood what that meant. She then told the kids that they were going to butcher it. These "McDonald's kids" were horrified. She shook her head. They were horrified. Kids today knew nothing about their food.

She watched for my reaction and then lowered her voice, telling me a story about a kid at the local school whose father was called a "murderer" because he was a pig farmer. The kid had gone home crying. She sat and stared hard at me. Would I be more of the same? I could feel her resentment. Like those kids in school and at the sports field, I needed to think about my lack of knowledge. Marie was warning me that a deep gulf separated outsiders and ranchers. Outsiders were lost in television and fast food. Warning given, Marie wished me luck with my writing, smiled, and let me out the kitchen door.

I walked around the house to where JoAnne was unloading her cow horse, Snipper, from her trailer. He backed out faster than any horse I've ever seen, his hooves flinching as if he were stepping on fire. Others were unloading their horses, and one guy revved up his four-wheeler, not an uncommon tool for rounding up cattle. JoAnne noticed that I was looking at the four-wheeler. She climbed up on her horse and joked around about how horses were still needed on the range.

I was left standing on the ground, horseless, with my camera in my hand. They all had talked before I showed up, deciding they couldn't afford to have a greenhorn scatter the cows, though I had never asked to ride. In my mind I was protecting my camera. In theirs I was a potential liability. The day's work had to go right, and no unnecessary chances would be taken. Even though I had ridden horses most of my life, my work with cows was virtually nil, and I was old enough not to pretend. Someday I'd like to round up cows—I've seen too many Westerns not to have the urge—but today I was content to walk and take pictures, sit on a hill and catch the action.

Anyway, I liked the way these cow horses act. The way they stared down a cow and danced it back to the herd. Intense and nimble, they would target a stray and not let go. Even the most belligerent cow could not shake off a good cow horse. The horse seemed to read the mind of the cow and anticipate where it wanted to run. And they were always there first, pushing the cow back to the herd.

Before they took off to find the cattle, Les had asked JoAnne if I'd expected him to look like a cowboy. He didn't have leather chaps on, and he wore a ragtag collection of working clothes. I told him I had met plenty of ranchers who wore sneakers and baseball caps, so he shouldn't worry. His face lit up, and in that cold morning light, he recited from his horse a cowboy poem he had written about a roping contest and a cowboy, all decked out in his best Western gear, who gets beaten by a guy with turtles on his shirt, sneakers on his feet, and a baseball cap on his head. His voice rang clear and melodious, each phrase crisply shaped, while his horse paced to the rhythm of his lines. When he finished, we laughed hard. Then they rode off, leaving me alone.

Once their horses had disappeared behind a hill, the weight of the emptied horizon settled on my mind. I felt uneasy. I was a stranger here. The hard-packed earth of this frosty October morning felt like concrete beneath my boots. Standing next to the vacant corrals, I heard ducks streak overhead, the sounds of their wings interrupting the stillness of the air and my worried thoughts. Pointed like arrows, they headed straight for a small pond tucked in a draw about 200 yards away. I had never heard this sound before—the rhythmic shushing of wind.

I walked over to the pond and its flurry of ducks to find relief from the parched, open range. There was no easy way to get to the water's edge, which was overgrown with willows and swampy with reeds. After a few attempts to break through the brush, I gave up, stood back, and only imagined what it would be like to sit next to the cool water and feel the protection of the trees. The arid landscape had already begun to make me thirsty, and I regretted not having brought along more drinking water. I spotted a knoll in the distance and headed toward its rise, a place to watch and wait for JoAnne and her friends to return.

The harshness of this land cost those who ranched here and still tried to make a living. JoAnne pieced together work as a hired hand for friends who themselves barely scraped by. Her work kept her in the saddle. At seventy years of age, she still felt cattle ranching was what she knew best, even though she now lived in a trailer at the edge of a small town nearby.

A few days later, I would spend the morning with her at her home, cluttered with tools, horse gear, newborn kittens, and too much furniture. She seemed dwarfed in that cramped space. I still had images in my mind of her perched on the edge of a rise, trying to get a stray cow down and into the waiting corral beneath. Tense, the cow tried to take a stand but quickly gave up and headed down the slope with a new urge to rejoin the herd. JoAnne spun her horse around and dove after the cow to make sure it didn't change its mind. She looked magnificent.

In her trailer, JoAnne seemed restless, like she was thinking about cattle and how long it would take to get back outside. Her hair was still fixed in a single braid, and now I noticed thin streaks of gray lacing through its dark color. Indian-bead earrings framed her weathered face, and she talked while cupping a newborn kitten in her lap. I sat opposite her in an overstuffed chair. I wanted to know what rodeo meant to a woman who was still a cowgirl, but a cowgirl without a ranch. In the mid-1940s, JoAnne had been co-queen in a small rodeo in Colfax, Washington, and rodeo princess for the Lewiston Roundup. She had grown up on a ranch in southeastern Washington, and those years had set the pattern for her life. "I did not know anything else and I loved animals so I was right at home . . . Anything I could do with my dad, that's where I was. I was a tomboy. I knew how to fix fence and I knew how to do the things we had to do. We didn't have anything real nice. You had to fix it."

JoAnne was proud of her ability to repair her world. She had shunted aside traditional women's work for the chance to work outside with her dad. Luckily, she had found and married a man who would ranch with her along the Snake River. All that was gone now. What remained was her trailer, a few horses, a couple of cattle, and ranch work when she could get it.

Outside JoAnne's home were makeshift corrals, strung together with whatever was handy. Guinea hens ran under the gates; dogs and cats slept underneath sheds and curled up, tucked in the corners of stairs. JoAnne wanted to talk about cattle. She always hung onto a few, through good times and bad. She asked me how anyone could afford beef today, the prices being so high. "I mostly stayed in with the cattle 'cause its extra income for me 'cause I have a few cows and the cows are just extra. That way you kind of come out even . . . A few, not too many. It helps to have your own meat; I'm used to that. I don't know how people eat meat when they have to buy it over the market, it is so expensive. Of course, it's expensive your own too, but still and all you've got it and know what it is and you fatten it up so it's good meat."

When I started asking her questions about her years in rodeo, she looked uncomfortable. Her words were sparse and quick. How could she have imagined that fifty years later someone would ask about what it was like to be a rodeo queen? She laughed uneasily, saying she should have taken notes. For some women, talking about the rodeo brought sadness. Flipping through their crumbling rodeo scrapbooks with black-and-white photos whose glue had long ago disintegrated, several women actually turned away, unwilling to look at their young faces. Others sighed over the impossibility of time. Now the doctor bills and medications lined their bathroom cabinets and kitchen counters, reminding them of illnesses, hip-replacement surgery, and vanished friends. Rodeo reminded them of their own decay.

For JoAnne, talking about rodeo brought back its thrills and excitement. Like Maxine, she saw rodeo as a break from the monotony of hard ranch work. "We lived on a ranch and we didn't have very much money," she explained. "We would go to a movie now and then or go to town and buy groceries. That's why it seems so funny to me for the kids to complain that they're bored. I say, 'How can you be bored? You got everything.' . . . [On the rodeo court] I was doing something I had never even thought of doing." When she was princess in Lewiston, the rodeo board took her "to a nightclub deal way up on the river. Don't remember exactly where it was. But we went clear up the river. It was a club. It was *really* nice. We had dinner there."

JoAnne loved every minute of her time as rodeo princess. "It was about the highest thing I ever did besides get married. Really it was." She was quick to add that it was pure fun—it had nothing to do with the reality of ranching. The connection between rodeo events like calf roping or bronc riding and ranching was a pure fantasy to her. In rodeo, "they generally either are bulldogging cows or either riding bulls or roping calves and throwing them." But JoAnne had grown up on ranches that used corrals and squeeze chutes to herd, house, and organize their cattle for branding, vaccinations, and castrations. "We did our cows in corrals. There are ranches that rope and did it all out on the range. We didn't do that. We weren't quite that rough." No one wanted to run down a cow or spend much time roping one. Running makes the cow lose weight, and weight equals money. Roping can injure cattle and was only to be used in emergencies. JoAnne would try at all costs to avoid throwing an animal, wanting her cows docile and unafraid of human hands.

The difference in horse handling was even more extreme. On the ranch, there was absolutely no bucking, she insisted. "No, no, I just like to have those horses a little bit gentle. . . . Daddy used to break horses and my brothers did. They tried not to let them buck. They just worked with them." How could you ever want a horse to buck when you had to depend upon it, sometimes with your life? How silly. Only rodeos would make bucking a game. "We used to like to watch the cowboys ride the bucking horses. It was something I didn't do, but I liked to watch it." Rodeo cowboys played in an arena, didn't work on a ranch. Anyone could tell the difference.

But contemporary rodeo promoters did not want to tell the difference. I wondered what JoAnne thought about the promotional hype on television, in newspapers, flyers, and official programs distributed at rodeos throughout the United States. They repeated nonstop the tired clichés of how rodeo reflected ranching and America's heroic pioneer past. Rodeo was the ultimate American sport because it linked historical truth and athletic prowess.

Even more, rodeo promoters touted the rodeo as a forum for all-American values. The pastoral world of the ranch evoked values such as hard work, tenacity, and bravery, and by the magic of association, the rodeo supposedly reflected these values, too. Once the connection was made, the rodeo became a morality play acting out our national destiny. A recent book on rodeo ended with this bold statement: "As we move forward toward a new century, we hope that Americans will continue to view rodeo as the keeper of an American tradition that, though it spanned only a brief period in history, remains forever a part of this country's core values and its soul." I think JoAnne would have laughed. Rodeo was an escape from the realities of ranching, not the keeper of a national tradition.

Until the last fifteen or twenty years, there was some truth to the link between rodeo and ranching. Rodeo performers usually lived in the rural West and often worked at least part-time on ranches. Hired hands, tenant ranchers, and children from small towns would travel down the rodeo road and try their luck for a few years in the high-risk world of rodeo. But most family-owned ranches could not spare their sons for the rodeo world. Joining the rodeo was a little like joining the circus; it might give you an adrenaline rush, but it hardly got the cattle branded or put food on the table.

This pool of performers declined as rodeo turned professional and succumbed to the pressures of specialization. The urban-raised bull riders of today's rodeo have little or no connection to the ranching life. To the shock of old rodeo fans, many had never ridden a horse. They even sell off the Western saddles they win as part of their prize. What are they going to do with them? Hang them in the garage next to their new to-die-for pickup truck?

Part of the confusion over rodeo's connection to the ranch stems from the varied styles of ranching found throughout the United States. Terry Jordan makes a strong case that there are at least three overlapping cattle cultures in America, arising from widely different roots: southwestern Iberia, the British highlands, and the sub-Saharan steppes of West Africa.

JoAnne's cattle culture is closest to that of the British high-lands—cows are kept docile before they are shipped to market. In contrast, Mexico and the southwestern United States tended to follow Iberian traditions, running down cows, especially wild cows. This technique was practiced in the early nineteenth century when hides, not meat, were sold in market. Rather than rope cattle, vaqueros chased and cut the cow's hamstrings with sharp, curved knives. The cow would fall in its own blood. The hide was taken but the meat was left to rot, consumed by scavengers. Before the Civil War, New England shoe factories depended upon the trade with hides that were picked up along the California coast and shipped back by boat to New England. In *Two Years Before the*

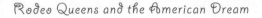

Mast, Richard Henry Dana, Jr. recounts the hours he sat next to stacks of hides drying in the sun, waiting for ships to pick up their precious cargo along what he considered the uninhabitable coast of California.

Such trade in hides was gradually phased out when cavalry, horsemen, miners, and settlers out West began to demand meat. Cattle barons began moving large herds of cattle for human consumption, especially after the Civil War. Since Native Americans were often forbidden to hunt, Indian reservations were a quick market for commodity beef provided through government contracts. In the nineteenth century, the hide and cattle business were hardly the domain of the independent owners or laborers, the idealized rugged individual of national myth. In fact, the late nineteenth century witnessed the creation of enormous ranches like the 3-million-acre XIT ranch in Texas, owned by the Capital Syndicate, a Chicago consortium.

Rodeo promoters usually avoid talking about the big-business side of the cattle industry, preferring to glamorize the heroic cowboy or cowgirl unattached to corporate greed. In the rodeo arena, ranch work was cut away from this century-long conflict over the ownership and control of Western lands. The simple, primitive labor of the cowboy working with horse, cattle, and bulls became a pastoral image of a time before the taking of Western lands by syndicates, corporations, and banks. The conflicts over who had the right to land were forgotten once the rodeo cowboy danced.

Maybe JoAnne had the right idea. She refused to see politics and symbols in rodeo because the rodeo was not the ranch, period. It did not reflect America's past or its future. Rodeo was merely fun, a break from the daily grind of ranch drudgery. Why spoil it with all that moral weight and national purpose? As rodeo royalty, she had a chance to do something she had never thought of doing. She could dress up, go to town, and meet people outside the world of cattle and wheat. Her social world opened up when she became royalty. Riding in parades, going to dinners, and traveling to nearby communities to promote the rodeo provided a break from the social isolation and obscurity of ranch life. JoAnne also felt the glow of pride at having been singled out and recognized for what she could do on her horse. Someone had noticed.

In the years JoAnne has lived in rural Washington, she has seen an entire world disappear, and I do not mean that as a metaphor. No, her world has actually disappeared, vanished beneath tons of water. In mid-century, demands for cheap electricity from aluminum corporations, urban growth, and irrigation projects reshaped the landscape of the interior Northwest. Responding to the need for energy, the government came in and built dams. The dams flooded out ranches, orchards, and sacred Indian sites. At the time, JoAnne was living with her first husband on a ranch along the Snake River, a place that became famous because an ancient human skeleton, known as "Marmes man," was found in a cave along the riverbank. This discovery made the flooding a news event.

JoAnne dug out the old newspaper clippings from stacks of papers on her kitchen table. She was still excited about the Lewis and Clark medal found at the site, probably presented to the local Indians in the early nineteenth century as a sign of peace and goodwill. Her voice was calm when she explained what had happened. "We had an irrigated ranch and we built up a little herd of cows and raised alfalfa. Eventually the Corps [Army Corps of Engineers] came in and bought us out and we didn't have a place.

That's when Lower Monumental Dam went in and flooded everything. I have pictures of it when the water was coming up."

Archaeologists had been working in the area on a nearby ranch. "They had dug out some caves on McGregor [her neighbor] and they knew the Indians had used the caves and then they came down to our place and wanted to know if they could dig that cave out. My husband told me he didn't care if they wanted to. So they set up and that's where they found the oldest Marmes. They called the cave Marmes Rock Shelter . . . They put a dam in but it didn't hold. They didn't get clear down to rock and [the water] came in faster than they could keep it out. They lined the holes that they had dug. They lined them with Visqueen [sturdy plastic sheeting] and filled them full of sand so it's still there like that. They always thought they might maybe come back in. I don't know. . . . We went up on the hill and eventually we broke apart and I went to work and worked ever since."

The building of Lower Monumental Dam on the Snake River, part of a series of dams constructed by the Army Corps of Engineers, buried JoAnne's world under the controlled waters of a hydrologist's vision of the West. After that, she divorced and worked odd jobs at whatever she could find. When JoAnne told me this story, I remembered how my former father-in-law used to laugh when he was playing a losing hand of cards and say, "The whole ranch is under water." He had fled the parched lands of Oklahoma and worked for a steel company that made the huge gates for several dams on the Snake. The dams promised to create jobs, ensure economic growth, and sustain agricultural development. For a while they did, but not without horrific costs that are still fiercely debated today, including the loss of salmon habitat. Environmental destruction was pitted against economic and agricultural interests. The small ranchers lost in the equation.

JoAnne thumbed through the curling newspaper clippings and

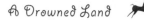

pointed to the wall by the side of her trailer door. All that remained of her Snake River ranch was an old black-and-white photo hanging on her imitation-wood-paneled wall. Her ranch could not survive a postwar economy that demanded hydroelectric power. JoAnne had lived in a West with monumental dreams controlled by concentrated capital. Holding onto a couple of cows on a couple of acres next to a trailer was all that was left of her dream to "own it all."

Many historians of the West have documented how corporate moneys, railroads, federal land-resource policies, domestic and foreign mineral extraction, harsh environmental conditions, and raw human greed have worked to destroy the self-sufficient, pastoral ideal of the ranch. Ranchers were never independent; the land and its resources were always linked to national markets and global financial cycles. The arid and eerily beautiful landscape of the Snake River was not spared. Its riverbanks were cut and reshaped by the force of politics.

JoAnne was not the only one to see her ranch disappear under advancing waters. For decades, Palouse Indians had fought over the right to ranch along the river's bank. In the 1920s, white ranchers like the McGregors, JoAnne's neighbors to this day, testified for Indian homesteads and their right to remain rather than be forced to take allotments on reservations in various parts of Washington, Idaho, and Oregon. Other whites fought to claim any available lands that Indians not living on reservations still worked. Conflicts over land titles, homesteads, and reservation allotments made ownership an ongoing legal and political battle along these crusty and rattlesnake-infested shores. Law courts rather than guns became the dominant way for race relations and land claims to find their strained settlements.

When Ice Harbor Dam was built in the 1950s on the Snake River, several miles from Lower Monumental Dam, Palouse Indians like Mary Jim, who had hung onto their land in order to fish and tend ancestral graves despite constant pressure from white ranchers and farmers, witnessed Lake Sacajawea flood out their homes and burial plots. As Mary Jim explained, before the dams, the river "played music" to her people's ears even after years of fighting off the newly arrived settlers along the shore. The dam was the final act of desecration. The water became voiceless, dead silent. The river had stopped singing.

Every inch of land where JoAnne has lived shares this political history. Most people have packed up and moved away. They found jobs in the cities or reluctantly moved to reservations and thought about what could have been. Some like JoAnne and Mary Jim stayed and fought, living a life reduced to the bone, making their own compromises with politics and history. After the trauma of dislocation, they tried everything they could to stay on the land, even if it meant poverty and hardship.

When I started to leave JoAnne's trailer, she walked with me outside where her horses were munching on some yellowing hay. She had pieced together her corrals from old fence posts, wire, and salvage lumber. She had made do with what had come her way. We talked horses in the cold air. Without hesitation, JoAnne offered to help me find a new horse, maybe even a good cow pony with whom I could have some fun. She meant it.

Our conversation came to a quick halt when a young couple drove up fast in their white pickup. They had come to ask JoAnne to help them hang a fence gate. JoAnne glanced at me, then dashed back into her trailer to grab her jacket and a few tools. She said a hurried good-bye. There was work to be done.

I stood there watching as the pickup raced away. Guinea hens perched on the railings and the horses in the corral stared at me, waiting for my next move. I hesitated before getting back in my car. I was remembering an old black-and-white snapshot my parents

still had tucked away in a family album. I was a child, maybe eight years old, walking in the Garden of Gods, near Colorado Springs, hauling a large red rock back to our waiting Buick. A child fed on Westerns who had stared out the car window for three days, pressed in the corner of a back seat, I was anxious for the thrill of mountains and the West of my dreams. The rock was much too large for my small hands. I wanted more than I could hold. I could barely lift it.

Seconds after this photo was taken, I remember the rock was returned to rest inside the park. "Leave it the way it was," my mother said. We drove off, and I was left with red clay on my hands and the disappointment of losing. I wanted to possess the land and make it mine. It was a child's dream, a child unaware that someone else called the land home already, someone else had the power to control it, and someone else would gamble it for their own bankrolled schemes.

Every year throughout the United States, the rodeo plays out a pastoral vision of the premodern West. It keeps alive a dream that has always been complicated by race relations, politics, land, and capital—the dream of possessing and working the land. Yet the dream persists. It's told again and again through national stories about American identity. And through those stories, the ranch lives on, even if it's long gone. JoAnne witnessed its disappearance, though she never used rodeo as a way to hold onto her memories. Tenacious, she kept her connection to ranching by doing odd jobs and keeping a few cows. She lives for her chance to get back on her horse and do what she knows best. Her two years as rodeo royalty were an early escape from incessant labor and an opportunity to play cowgirl apart from the struggle of holding onto the land. But the land remained the magnet, the place where she felt alive and at home.

That is the problem: Who has the right and the power to own

and control this land? We have not even begun to settle that basic question in the West, let alone what responsibilities come with ownership. Maybe rodeo is like a piece of candy. A sweet taste that comes and goes. Tempting and teasing, it distracts us from the politics of where we live. It tries to satisfy the hunger that drives this land, but it never lasts. Its peoples are still left fighting over who belongs.

4

Trusting the Wild

When I returned from traveling in central China during the summer of 1994, the first thing I did was hike up the East Lostine River toward Minam Peak in the Eagle Cap Wilderness Area in the northeast corner of Oregon. I was on the trail for nearly an hour when I came to a bend in the river that branched out through marshy terrain covered with yellow wildflowers, stream violets, and columbines. The bend shaped the water into a deeper pond, a crystalline quarter moon. The water, a pale blue-green jade, glowed with the soft morning light. The color anchored me in place. The water made the world make sense.

I was suffering from a deprivation of water. For the entire summer in China, I had seen only the brackish ruins of waterways, thick with pollutants from a society racing to catch up and stake a place on the global playing board. Every day I boiled my water or poured hot water from a communal boiler into a tall metal thermos. I had known about bad water before, having grown up near the Chicago River, a sludgy channel that suffered the further indignity of being dyed green for St. Patrick's Day. My life span coincided with growing fears about the demise of the Great Lakes and horror stories of fires from industrial waste on Lake Erie, but with over a billion people, China's pollution was on a scale beyond my comprehension.

I sat and gazed at the water for a long time. I had walked up this river to see if I could understand again where I lived. China's race to create a modern industrial nation-state had made me think about our own national race toward progress and its effects on our communities, forests, and waterways. I needed a reprieve from the hard facts of life in a hyperdeveloped globe, and I came to the Lostine River to regain my perspective.

I struggled to find my balance. I felt the need for a steady diet of wilderness to keep away the demons of modernity. I became a backpacking tourist, trying to find health on whatever week or weekend off I could find. Since the nineteenth century, the American West has been advertised as a healing and recreational oasis, a part of our national story about renewal and regeneration. Its wildness is seen as a counterpoint to our urban frenzy, a tonic for our modernizing ills. I soaked up the woods, seeking solace, repeating a journey Americans have taken for decades.

A year later, I returned to eastern Oregon and interviewed several local queens. I wondered if rodeo was another way to keep wildness alive in a modern technological society. I knew that anthropologists had studied the rodeo and seen it as a way for humans to confront and tame the wild. In the rodeo arena, wild bulls and horses challenge human skill and ingenuity. The crowd cheers for those men who can withstand their terrible force. Other writers on spectator sports point out that all modern societies preserve archaic parts of their past to reassure them of their roots in a simpler, less artificial time, closer to nature. There are no machines in the rodeo arena. No computers, no race cars, no cell phones. Leather saddles, ranch animals, and cowboys prevail.

Only after my visit with Blanche, a rodeo queen in the 1940s, did I really begin to question rodeo's relationship to the wild. Standing in front of her neat-as-a-pin ranchette, I watched the glow off the mountains in the Lostine River Valley spread over the neighboring pines. Blanche's ranchette sat on five and one-half acres, kept green by irrigation pipes. The garden had old plows and ranching tools tucked under flowers. A dried-out saddle squatted near the house, a flowerpot waiting for sun.

At the end of my visit, I had tried to take some photos of Blanche with her horse in the pasture next to her house. Dressed in slim black jeans and a carefully ironed shirt, Blanche walked next to Rex, her Polish Arab, a lean, chestnut horse. She had rescued him from a hard life as a hunter's horse. He was suspicious of my camera and kept shying away. She brushed his forelock out of his eyes and stroked him on the neck to calm him. He was not buying it and wove nervously, straining the lead line. When I got the photos back from the developer, they were disappointing. Blanche, looking down, intent on her horse. Blanche, hidden behind the restless movement of Rex, her short, curly brown hair blurred by the motion. The moment was gone.

But Blanche stayed with me long after our visit together, despite the bad photos. When we sat in her living room, she was eager to talk. The sandpaper in her voice only punctuated what she had to say, giving it a shape, the sound of wind hard on a stubble field.

Blanche was on four rodeo courts in the late 1940s, three in Oregon—the Wallowa County Fair, the Elgin Stampede, and Chief Joseph Days—and one in Idaho, the Lewiston Roundup. She made a living for years working as a ranger and recreation specialist, riding horses into the nearby National Forest lands. Now retired, she still camps in the high mountains with her horse. In her late sixties, Blanche has lost none of her zest for riding. "I can be tired, just real tired, and after dinner go out and brush my horse and saddle him up and go for two hours. I have wonderful places to ride back here in the hills after you get off the road, and then when the mountains open up. I just jump in the trailer and take off."

The Wallowas are where Blanche rides with her friends, even though each year brings changes to her mountain valley. "We don't have the places where we can ride like we used to have. It is all locked up or no trespassing signs are just everywhere. We can still ride in the mountains. When you get up there it's fresh and it's clean. You can see for miles. I just really can't put it in words." Blanche has had two hip-replacement surgeries and rides in a specially made orthopedic saddle. She had to go through a number of doctors before she found one who understood her need to ride.

She's clear about how her family and the ranch shaped her life. "I've been riding horses since I was old enough to get on a horse. I was my Dad's right hand. I did the wrangling and drove . . . We didn't have all this modern equipment. Everything was team horses. We did have a tractor. But mostly it was team horses. I had one brother. My brother didn't care for it [ranch work].. . . When it came time to bring the cattle in, we did a lot of exchange work. We helped our neighbors put their hay up. They helped us put our hay up. And that's sort of the way we did it then."

Blanche had few luxuries when she was young, but she had her horses. "My first pony we called Jenny Belle. She was just a good all-around horse. The reason she got the name Jenny Belle was I wanted to name her Jenny, and my brother wanted to name her Belle. My mother said, 'We will settle it. We'll name her Jenny Belle.' Good all-around horse, good cow sense, and she really wanted to please. I must have been around six. . . . We rode our horses to school. I really enjoyed it."

Growing up on stock ranches in Reva, South Dakota, and later in both Cayuse and Joseph, Oregon, Blanche loved rodeo. She was mesmerized by the trick riders and tried to imitate their stunts. "I ruined a good cow horse. I went down to the lower field. I wanted to be a trick rider and I took and taught her to rear by clenching my legs on her and pulling the reins. I remember that W. B. was riding that horse and he went to open the gate. And he leaned over to unlatch the gate and clenched his legs and pulled the horse back and the horse went straight up and he knew exactly what had happened. I got a spanking over that and I was a pretty good-size girl. I never forgot that." Rearing was not the only trick she tried outside her parents' watchful eyes. "I would stand up on her and ride until I fell off."

I had heard this story before from other rodeo queens—how they secretly tried to teach their horse tricks outside of their parents' scrutiny. The reaction was always the same. Extra work chores and privileges taken away. The domesticated ranch and the wildness of the rodeo were totally separate and incompatible, especially when it came to horses. Horses were unpredictable enough. When you tried to open a gate on horseback and pulled back on the reins, would you want your horse to rear up? A rancher's life struggle was to hedge in danger, to fight back wildness, not encourage it.

Pushing back her large eyeglasses, Blanche shook her head. She had strong feelings about the right way to handle horses and stressed the need to understand who a horse was. "They can feel you. They can sense by your tone of voice if you like them, if you are sincere about liking them," she said. "Then you get their trust and they will do anything for you. I just never had any horses that were kickers or biters because I work with them easy and slow, and never ever have I abused them. Firm but kind. Because they have to also know I'm not going to get away with this. I have to do this and so I am going to do it the easy way. They have to like what they're doing, too. And so if you work with them right, then they enjoy what they're doing, and you get so much more out of them. It's just a sheer joy. That's what I think."

It had taken Blanche years to understand horses. She grew up knowing the Dorrance family and read and reread Tom Dorrance's book on communication between humans and horses. Like Monty Roberts, author of *The Man Who Listens to Horses*, Dorrance was part of a new wave of male horse trainers whose style ran counter to the rough ways of the cowboy. Cowboys buck out horses to break them. These trainers listen to their animals, and respond to them. Tom Booker, the silent and sensitive protagonist of Nicholas Evans's *The Horse Whisperer* brought public attention to this new, male style of communication, in which man and horse are receptive and constantly aware of each other.

In the movie version of the book, Robert Redford slipped easily into the role of the sensitive male horse trainer. His portrayal reminded me of stories José Limón, an anthropologist, told in the mid-1980s about a peculiar version of the devil, who appeared to Mexican-American women in South Texas bars. This devil looked just like Redford. He caused much trouble among Mexican-American men, who saw him as a laughable but annoying threat to their own masculinity. This new form of sensitive maleness cast aside dominance and power, replacing macho strength with gentle persuasion and a patient longing for intimacy. Women (and horses) found it irresistible.

Redford's performance and Dorrance's work reinforces Blanche's perception that horses are not objects to be trained by humans to submit to human will. And there is no breaking involved. Instead, horses decide from human voice and body language if they are going to work with humans. As Tom Dorrance explains, a horse needs to learn through experience whether to trust and respect a human. In fact, a human takes on an enormous

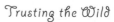

responsibility when entering into a relationship with a horse and needs to sustain and develop this respect and trust through count- less acts of touch, voice, and direction. Stephen Budiansky goes so far as to call the domestication of horses "a slow process of mutual adaptation" or "co-evolution." He argues that for thousands of years horses sheltered near human dwellings, gaining food and protection from their natural predators such as mountain lions and wolves. Horse and human tamed each other.

Blanche agreed with this philosophy of horsemanship. She learned an early version from her father. "My dad was a real horse- man. We had a stallion on the place and we raised our own. He could read horses. He studied them." She also remembered that when she was young, taming a horse meant confrontation between humans and horses, and that rodeo glamorized this approach. "Back then they trained horses so differently. They immediately would get on them and buck them out. They wanted to get the buck out." Blanche's technique was entirely different. "The last horse I trained was from a colt. About eight years ago. I did my groundwork and the horse trusted me and I knew just about what the horse would do. I used a round corral. The horse never ever bucked. I saddled it. I ponied [trained] it. . . . You have to be in synch with your horse all the time to really be a real horseman." It was a long-range view; nothing happened quickly. Time was stretched out as an endless learning curve, and humans had to let go of conventional ideas of power and control in order to relate to animals.

The rodeo cowboy saw things differently. Those I have talked with often described the bucking-horse contests as an elaborate dance, involving the unpredictability of the horse in a structured situation, the experience, knowledge, and technique of the rider, and the know-how of the crew who handle the horse in the chute, prepare the ride, and pick up the rider at the end. The goal is to get in synch with the horse and spur in such a way as to create a high-bucking ride.

In fact, artificial aids are used to encourage bucking, such as the flank strap that is fastened over the back and under the stomach of the horse during the bucking contests in the rodeo. Supposedly, the strap makes the horse feel as though it has something on its back and sets off an instinctual fight-or-flight response. The flank strap helps to make the horse buck. It is detached immediately at the end of a ride. To Blanche, the strap symbolized the betrayal of a relationship between man and horse. Even though she felt overall that the horses and cattle in the rodeo were much better cared for than in her youth, she still thought the rodeo rested upon inappropriate means to achieve its ends. At some basic level, the rodeo ruined the relationship humans can have with the horse. Rodeo was a one-way street with humans seeking control and power. Taming meant submission.

She knew well that stock contractors—the men and women who provide the animals for the rodeo—are quick to point out that rodeo animals are the pampered, even spoiled, property of owners who feed them well, make sure their health is excellent, and nurture their every need. No wonder the contractors grow angry when animal-rights protesters accuse them of cruelty. From their point of view, they are caretakers. They work around the clock to maintain the animals, and the animals only have to perform for eight seconds.

Having lived in the rodeo world for years, Blanche was careful in her criticism. Rather than attack the rodeo directly, she kept insisting on the need to reexamine how we treat horses in general. She was aware that the treatment of animals in the rodeo arena was a hot topic, since animal-rights activists had been picketing rodeos in the last few years. She also understood why a bucking bronco, no matter how well fed, bucked to resist the spur and the flank strap. The horse was forced to fight human control.

From sitting behind the chutes at dozens of rodeos, I know the controversy over the treatment of rodeo animals extends well beyond the flank strap. From my seat in the stands, I know the rodeo simulates the wild through artificial techniques. It is mainly smoke and mirrors. Bulls are penned in tight quarters, agitated, girdled, and then often shocked with a bolt of electricity to insure they act mad and kick like hell. The walls of the chutes drip with nervous green shit. Rodeo clowns further confine, confuse, and irritate the animals until the eight-second ride is over. Without such artificial simulation, many bulls are calm and docile. Some need a ton of encouragement to look and act wild. Bucking horses are not that different. Sure, some are outlaws—problem horses who resist human training or, more likely, horses ruined by what passed as training— but most need the flank strap and the excitement of the chute, crowd, and spurs to buck and act wild.

I have also noticed how the audience responds differently to each rodeo event. Walking out is part of the rodeo experience. Men often walk out when the barrel racing starts. They do not see how women riding horses around barrels involves any real risk. What kind of sport is that? Too domestic. A few women walk out on bull riding. They feel rodeo is not a blood sport and recklessness should not be encouraged. Too wild. Men and women both walk out on team and calf roping. It's too boring for some—time to get a beer—and too cruel for others. The running down of doe-eyed calves rankles their sensibilities. It's too close to the butcher's knife. But most stay for the bucking-horse events, since the men are brave and seem to have half a chance, and the horses are rarely hurt; annoyed, yes, but hurt, no. Put at the end of the program, the bucking-horse and bull-riding events galvanize the crowd. Blood and danger (but not too much blood or too much danger) cut through the air.

Rodeo as a spectator sport shows the excitement of taming the wild by controlling animals for brief, intense moments of time. To these ends, humans need the help of other animals, horses in particular. In the rodeo, bucking horses and writhing bulls are only part of the show. Horses also serve as partners with rodeo cowboys in events such as calf roping and team roping, demonstrating how human-animal teams can work efficiently and skillfully to manipulate cattle.

Rodeo also maps our relationships with domestic animals, an essential part of our economy. We butcher and profit from bulls, steers, calves, and horses, and we entertain ourselves by competing with them in an invented game. Human bravery, courage, and pain are rewarded by money and applause. The costs to the animals are minimized in the arena—so much so that it is more acceptable for a rodeo cowboy to snap his back than for a horse to break a bone, go down, and suffer before the crowd. We forbid the public pain of animals in the arena even though we depend on them for daily food.

A contrast might be useful. Almost all rodeo people I have met, whether rodeo queens or not, despise bullfighting. Bullfighting, an entertainment form with strong parallels to rodeo, is embraced and defended in Spain, Portugal, Mexico, and several South American countries but has never established itself in North America, even though the word *rodeo* comes from the Spanish word meaning "to round up," and in the Southwest and southern California, *charreadas*, rodeos with Mexican traditions, continue to this day.

The killing of an animal in a public arena would find intense opposition in the United States. Similarly, when an animal is injured in the rodeo arena, the rodeo comes under heavy criticism. In the rodeo, animals can be dominated and controlled temporarily, but their sacrifice for our food and profit must never be made visible. In fact, successful bulls and bucking horses often become heroes in their own right. Living legends of the rodeo cowboy world, they are praised because no one can stay the ride, not even for eight seconds. No one can tame their wildness.

The rodeo avoids at all cost the pain and blood of animal sacrifice. Instead, it plays a game in which the pastoral values of ranch work with its Western work ethic are applauded while the consequences and power structures of this labor are obliterated.

Once in a while, the economic system shines through. In the movie *City Slickers,* the glamour of the cowboy lifestyle rubs against the reality of the cowboy's job. After Billy Crystal and his two buddies prove their manliness by trailing a herd of cattle to their final destination, they recognize that the effort was all about making hamburgers. This conflict does not reappear in the sequel. The ending of the initial movie downplays the inevitable sacrifice of the cattle by having Billy Crystal adopt one calf and bring it home to a fantasized life in New York, or, I would imagine, the suburbs, that space where many middle-class Americans still try to flee frightful conflicts. But Americans are not about to begin adopting calves. Instead, they get to enjoy a film about the male ritual of herding cattle and playing cowboy and then feel good when Billy does the right thing and rescues one sweet calf from the butcher's knife.

In the cultural pantomime of rodeo, men are seen as heroes in control of the wild for brief moments of time. Only when they break an arm or a leg or are crunched in the groin does the audience wonder about the costs of the pageantry. Part spectacle, storytelling, charade, celebration, theater, and show business, rodeo delivers its concept of the wild to a screaming crowd. Who would come to see Blanche's vision of working with horses for years before trust and respect emerge? Where would the thrill be? Rodeo audiences want the exhilaration of the unpredictable. They want adrenaline and fear. They want to be shaken from their tame lives and feel the quick pulse of danger.

Blanche felt uncomfortable about the frenzy of rodeo fans. She wanted people to see a different relationship between man and animal, one based on mutual respect, knowledge, and the commitment of time. The wildness and aggression that rodeo promotes ran against her sense of a livable world. Besides, the rodeo wasn't really wild. It hawked a sideshow imitation of wildness for a pumped-up crowd. Blanche's dance with horses came after years of give and take, fear and trust. No eight-second ride could come close to that thrill.

Every year, Blanche rides in the rodeo parade in Joseph, Oregon. I watched her march down Main Street on Rex, her beloved chestnut horse, during the fiftieth anniversary of Chief Joseph Days, the annual July rodeo in this small town tucked at the entrance to the Eagle Cap Wilderness Area. Though stiff in her knees and hips, she sat tall. She never flinched when the sound of the local high-school band made her horse start prancing and swerving. Blanche supported her community rodeo and still loved to dress up in her Western best for the celebration. The rodeo was part of her hometown, and she was part of the rodeo. "I ride in the Chief Joseph Days parade ever year because I am here. It's tradition, and heavens, I know practically everybody, even a lot of them that come from California, Tri-Cities, and that have come every year."

Like many others in this community who have doubts about the practices of rodeo, Blanche still supports the community spirit behind this annual event. People renew friendships through picnics, parties, and dances. Tourism booms during this weekend, and local businesses enjoy a momentary respite from the hard months of making a go of it during most of the year.

For many in the town, the rodeo is about staying Western and keeping connected to the past. For others, it is plain business, a needed source of income. For Blanche, fifty years of memories are wrapped up in this celebration of a few days. "Over all these years I have kept in touch with a lot of the pickup men, the court members, and so many people were so helpful to me. When I rode in the Lewiston Roundup, Chief Joseph Days, and the Elgin Stampede, you made friends that you still have as friends." Like many cultural rituals, the rodeo's repetition is its strength. One year is compared with the next; individual rides and cowboys are measured against each other. In some ways, the community knows itself through the local rodeo. It is central to the collective identity of this small town.

But all these good memories did not wash away more worries Blanche had about rodeo. Besides her questions about bucking horses, she had grown concerned about how the rodeo queen is selected. Something about it did not seem right. It wasn't right when she was young, and it still wasn't right today.

When Blanche was trying out for Chief Joseph Days royalty in the 1940s, she was asked to sell tickets to the event, something her mother felt was not an appropriate activity for a young woman. "Mother felt that it should be on you. You're selected on scholastic, horsemanship, personality, the type of person you were. She said, 'You just do not buy yourself.' That's the way she felt." In the 1940s, the girl who sold the most tickets was designated queen. Period.

Fifty years later, a version of this method of selection still holds true. The local newspaper and some people in the town have continued to criticize the selling of tickets as a major criterion for selection of the queen. Their criticism is not well received. When the newspaper printed an editorial asking for changes in the queen selection process, local businessmen yanked their ads. They were backed by the Chamber of Commerce, which considered the queen to be not only a promoter of the event but an active saleswoman who should go door-to-door, selling tickets to friends, family, community groups, and clubs. The community was divided. To some, the queen was supposed to be a model citizen, the best the town had to offer. To others, she was a marketing device, a mascot, a moneymaker.

Other rodeo queens and princesses from the 1940s and 1950s questioned the blatant commercialization of the rodeo today. Money had tainted the hometown feel of the event, they said. It no longer felt as though the entire community was pitching in to pull the celebration off. Instead, it all seemed to be about dollars. Who really controlled the rodeo, and who profited from it? Certainly, control over the local rodeo was connected to larger market forces. The local rodeo board negotiated not only with the local Western-wear stores but also with the corporate sponsors, such as Justin Boots, Coors, Budweiser, and Dodge trucks. Rodeo had gone from no business to local business to big business.

But keeping the rodeo clear of money conflicts would not be easy, since rodeo's history was all about how people worked and played, and how they lived on the land and lost. Rodeo started late in the nineteenth century when the farm and ranch were losing out to the factory and town. The flight from rural lands would result in an urban and industrial population. Farm and ranch children tried to get work in stores and in the professions, hoping to get into the emerging middle class. Instead, many became trapped in the working class, laboring in factories and small shops next to immigrants from Europe and the American South. In one sense, the rodeo celebrated the world of working with land and animals these people had left behind.

Compared to industrial workers, the rodeo cowboy seemed fearless and freed. This guy got to play. But he played according to certain rules. His ride was measured by the mechanical ticking of the industrial clock. The adrenaline rush of eight-second rides mimicked the frantic pace of modern life. Even though ranch rodeos had no time limits to saddle and ride wild horses, once in the arena, time limits became the norm. Ten-second rides shifted to eight in the late 1940s. In rodeo script, the lone cowboy pitted himself against the wild, submitted his labor to the demands of compressed time, and gambled his body to become a modern hero. He risked life and limb, competing against the clock. The rodeo simulated a Wild West before machines, factories, and urban sprawl, but like a Charlie Chaplin movie, it cranked up the speed at which the cowboy played, pushing his body into extreme pain.

The iconography of the rodeo cowboy on a bucking bull or horse was easily extracted from the rodeo and distributed on billboards, license plates, glassware, and the endless bric-a-brac of commercial goods. These cultural images propagated a neat lie: romantic cowboys ruled the West. Cowboys rocked. They got things done, fast. They didn't talk; they acted. The heroic labor of the cowboy was a cultural code, a slick surface over the complex manipulations of capital and power.

Not surprisingly, his simplified code became an international icon of American popular and political culture, popping up as the get-it-done cowboy diplomacy of the Cold War, floating around as images of cowboy country in the global commercialization of American products, and finding crowd appeal in the embossed cowboy boots of a new president, George W. Bush. Nameless and often faceless, the rodeo cowboy was a working-class action hero. Perhaps his most internationally recognized incarnation is as the Marlboro Man. The cigarette-smoking cowboy recently appeared as a rodeo bull rider pictured from the waist down with a close-up of his championship belt buckle glittering next to his lit match. This enormous image hung over stairwells to subways in Paris, Hong Kong, and New York. Thousands of harried urbanites each hour marched under his sweat-soaked jeans.

The rodeo queen is a less familiar stock character. She's the one who sells the show. And sell it she must. Like the rodeo cowboy, she is asked to represent a time when cash seemed less corrupt, when labor had more honor, and when the moral universe had a simpler axis upon which to spin. But cash sticks to the rodeo and its queen like flypaper. Try as she might to imagine a wild space infused with moral certitude, the mess of money runs the show.

Of course, my interpretation of rodeo history is irrelevant to most rodeo fans. It probably sounds like the paranoid academic vision of someone who has spent too much time thinking about rodeo and found more to critique than celebrate. Blanche would probably think I was crazy to even bring it up. How had I strayed from her worries about selling tickets to a wholesale blast at the rodeo show? She would probably laugh at me and suggest a long horse ride in the mountains.

Despite her own unease about the rodeo's message and its treatment of animals and rodeo royalty, Blanche never missed the parade. When I stood on the sidewalk for the fiftieth-anniversary rodeo parade, I waved as she rode past. I watched as her neighbors yelled out her name and clapped. She smiled back, urging Rex forward, encouraging him to enjoy the moment. Strong and resilient, Blanche had a clear role to play for her neighbors and friends. Sure there were doubts, but once a rodeo queen, always a rodeo queen.

5

Leaving Pocahontas

The Wildhorse Gaming Resort stands near the historic Oregon Trail, on which overlanders traveled 2,000 miles over 150 years ago to reach the rich soil of the Willamette Valley. The area is part of the Umatilla Indian Reservation. The resort's bold geometric architecture is edged with red diamond shapes, yellow chevrons, and turquoise bands that light up the surrounding plain. The flat plateau of the Columbia Basin stretches beyond the resort for miles, its surface interrupted by folds of sand-washed hills that eventually dissolve into the Blue Mountains. The plateau is like a giant bowl set down on earth to hold the sky.

Its desolate beauty vanishes as soon as you step through the casino's front door. Inside, the perpetually dark Las Vegas–style gaming room pulsates with the loud ringing of slots. The cavernous main hall is packed with day-trippers playing nickel machines. Side rooms offer higher-stakes board games for the adventurous who know more about the odds than bit players like me.

I had come early for my meeting with Leah in order to gamble. Determined to test my luck, I tried my hand at the silver slots, which rise like cool obelisks from the casino floor. Impulse told me to bet and bet quickly, but I had to wait in line. On this Saturday afternoon, every room in the casino was thick with people, their faces anxious and haggard. After a few impatient minutes, I stepped up to a vacated slot machine—the seat was still warm—and lost $20 in microseconds, not enough time to even enjoy the spinning of Native American gold-dollar signs.

Next to me, a woman placed her right hand on the electronic screen of her Dream Catcher machine and held it against the plastic surface for a few seconds. She concentrated, sending luck or maybe prayer through her fingertips before she released her hand and pushed the max-bet key. At another machine, I saw a miniature Jesus stuck on a narrow ledge beneath swirling columns of red, white, and blue bars.

The room spilled over with retired gray-haired ladies and their thinning husbands, frail but determined to gamble with what time they had left. Migrant workers, nervous and intense, spent their money quickly and got out. Hundreds of locals, clusters of tourists, and the occasional wanna-be Indians—whites dressed in braids and beads—watched the hypnotic dance of the spinning slots. Working class, middle class, and the unemployed mingled in this hall of improbability.

It was as if the machines were telling all of us: Hard work got you so far, but not out of debt, not out of the strain of monthly bills. In this dark room, we knew wealth was a game of chance or maybe a glance from the gods. For hours after my visit when I closed my eyes, I could still hear the staccato sounds of the casino—the clink-clink, clink-clink-clink-clink-clink of its slot machines—taunting me to test my luck.

After I emptied my wallet, I waited for Leah in front of the casino restaurant, the best place for lunch on the reservation, and tried to ignore the urge to pull out my credit card and head toward the ATM. Maybe next time. Then I spotted Leah walking through the crowd. I recognized her immediately, even though I had seen her only once before at the fiftieth reunion for rodeo royalty in Joseph, Oregon. Short, with a strong face punctuated by radiant dark eyes and a warm broad smile, she moved with a measured and dignified pace. She greeted me with a gentle handshake, then asked if I wanted to eat.

The frantic casino energy dissipated as I talked with her. Her calm and direct voice made me settle into my chair and listen. Leah wanted to know about my family first; not about what I did, but who I was and who my relatives were. I told her about the large, sprawling network of parents, siblings, cousins, nephews, and nieces who lived in Chicago, too far away. About my daughter and her life. She wanted to know how I came west, why I was living where I was. She listened carefully, her eyes never straying from my face. Few rodeo royalty I had talked with ever expressed interest in who I was as a person. Some were concerned that I was not a rodeo insider, but most never wanted to know about how I lived, whether I was a wife, mother, or daughter. They simply weren't interested.

Leah had brought along a beautiful black-and-white photograph of her maternal grandmother, Mrs. Spokane Jim, an Umatilla Indian. We talked about the words *Native American, Native people, American Indian,* and *Indian.* Leah preferred the term *Native American* when stressing sovereignty rights, but she understood that words played many roles. The term *Native American* could misrepresent tribes like the Okanogans, whose homeland was in both the United States and Canada. A tribal designation was best. I remembered heated debates with native writers to whom the word *Indian* was an act of defiance against the more politically correct *Native American.*

She placed the picture delicately on the table between us. Her grandmother's image stayed there for the rest of the conversation. Her piercing eyes stared out of the photograph, alert and unwavering. I wondered who took the photograph. I have spent many hours working on the photographs of Edward Sheriff Curtis, who, in the 1890s, recorded what he considered the dying remnants of a vanishing race. Curtis traveled the United States for twenty years capturing Indians on paper. Little did he know that his images would be used by the tribes to preserve their way of life rather than by a white audience to lament their passing.

As I looked at the photograph, Leah began to outline her genealogy, a web of connections tying her to Chief Joseph and his brother Alikut, members of the Willamootkin Clan and Wallowa Band of the Nez Perce whose lives were permanently scarred by war with the United States in 1877. Unlike other Nez Perce who signed an 1863 treaty with the United States ceding key tribal lands, these bands had never sold or ceded ownership of their traditional homeland, Wallowa Valley, in eastern Oregon. When violence erupted between white settlers and Nez Perce warriors in the Wallowas, General Oliver Otis Howard of the U.S. Army, a Civil War veteran, fought and pursued the nontreaty Nez Perce, intent on forcing them onto a small reservation created in 1863.

Rather than face confinement, Chief Joseph and his band fled to the Canadian border, hoping for refuge with Sitting Bull and his Sioux encampment. But they were stopped just short of the border after having fought four major battles in which 65 men and 55 women and children were killed. The remaining 418 Nez Perce were taken as prisoners of war to a camp near Fort Leavenworth, Kansas. They were never allowed to return to the Wallowa Valley. In that war, roughly between June 2 and October 5, Alikut, a war and hunting leader, died at the Bear Paw Battle in Montana.

As Leah spoke about her family's past, it was as if her ancestors crowded around her voice, listening. History to Leah was not required textbook reading, but a story alive with the deeds of loved ones whose memories lived on in their descendants. She told me her Indian name from her father's side was Tamikatcat, the sound of a swan's wings lifting into flight.

The muffled sounds of the casino spilled over her words. She paid no attention to the noise as she told me about her childhood. Raised on the Umatilla Indian Reservation, Leah's life had been filled with horses. Her maternal grandfather was a gambler and a horse trader. Her mother and aunt rode horses everywhere together and traveled with the seasonal migrations of the tribe as they hunted, gathered roots, and traded. Young people played horse games in the mountains where the strict eyes of their elders could not reach. When Leah was young, she and her siblings would ride horses barefoot in their summer clothes. They would camp at Cayuse Ridge and ride to the mountains in the warm months to a place called "Poverty Flat," a name imposed by people Leah called "emigrants"—whites who do not understand how local geography resonates with the tribes, their sacred places, and family stories. She still chafes at their power to name her home. She prefers the name Cabbage Hill to Poverty Flat because of the dense skunk cabbage that covers the ground in early spring.

Leah's brother was a calf roper when he was young, the "only one in the family to really get into horses," and her youngest daughter works as a horse trainer and manager. The two of them, niece and uncle, disagree on how to raise horses. Leah's daughter believes that horses have emotions and that a gentle training approach works best. Her brother believes more in authority and control. Leah said they both care deeply for their horses. She respects their right to disagree.

Leah was queen of the Pendleton Round-Up in 1952, and before that she served as an honorary Indian princess for Chief Joseph Days in Joseph, Oregon. As queen, she was selected by the rodeo committee to represent and promote the rodeo activities. As Indian princess, she was selected by her tribe to represent the tribe at the rodeo. Leah had good memories of her rodeo days, but she also had her points of criticism. In the 1940s and early 1950s, rodeo was mainly a local celebration. In those years, Leah explained, Indians "tried to do both." She thought Indians today "still do both, but in a different way."

I tried to understand what she was saying. When I questioned her, she was silent for a few moments and then continued, "Today not many Indians go to rodeos." Something had changed. The rodeo used to be a way to "do both"—to participate in both the Indian and white worlds—but Leah felt that it was not true for many Indians anymore. In the 1940s, Indians and whites played together at the rodeo, but times had changed. Indians still ride in the rodeo parade, set up their encampment, and hold a powwow, but they don't go to the rodeo. They are not the rodeo crowd. Rodeo was no longer the place to connect the two worlds. There were more significant bridges for Indians in education, business, and the arts. Sitting in the casino restaurant, Leah spoke clearly about the economic and cultural initiatives of the tribes. Their destiny was no longer shaped by the formulas of the Old West.

I had prepared for my meeting with Leah by reading as much as I could about the Pendleton Round-Up, one of the oldest rodeos in the United States. Set in the dryland country of north-central Oregon, Pendleton began its rodeo in the fall of 1910 when Roy Bishop of the Pendleton Woolen Mills, together with area ranchers and businessmen, invited the Umatilla, Walla Walla, and Cayuse Indians to participate. Many of Leah's ancestors were there at the very beginning, though Leah's mother and aunt missed the first roundup. They had not returned from their traditional summer-long gathering of food and hides in the mountains of eastern Oregon.

With the cooperation of the tribes, the rodeo grew more and more popular. Thousands of whites poured into this small town every September to watch the parade, Indian dances, Indian horse races, and rodeo events. The rodeo became a magnet for Indians throughout the region, and large Indian gatherings camped next to the rodeo grounds. Family and friends would use this time to eat, celebrate, and make extra money. The temporary village of teepees was a great draw for tourists, but it also provided time and space for Indians to gather, exchange news, eat food, gossip, and even trade.

In these early years, many local rodeos tried to have their own impromptu Wild West shows in which local Indians teamed up with whites to perform choreographed battles and "scenes" from the history of the West. Pendleton tried the Wild West format, but according to Virgil Rupp, the rodeo's historian, the local tribes would not participate in a staged battle "unless they could shoot back." As early as 1910, the local Indians resisted the tired formulas of the Wild West in which whites garnered sympathy because of staged Indian attacks on defenseless settlers' cabins. The Wild West shows justified white violence, arguing that whites needed to protect their homesteads and tame the West. The local Indians would not buy it. They refused to join the charade. By 1917, Wild West shows were on the decline throughout the United States. Movie companies took over many of the stock images, creating the hugely popular Western genre. Rodeos would have to carve out a somewhat different niche.

The Pendleton Round-Up tried a slightly different approach to the clichéd cowboy-and-Indian fare. In 1913, four years before Buffalo Bill Cody died, Pendleton produced a new type of Wild West show, known as Happy Canyon. Called "The Pageant of the West—an Outdoor Dramatic Production, Symbolizing the History and Development of the Great West," the show was usually considered the brainchild of Roy Raley, a Pendleton pioneer. But according to Leah, Happy Canyon was the product of the combined efforts of two people, Roy Raley and Anna Minthorn, an Indian woman who was also a Sunday school teacher at the Presbyterian church. Anna Minthorn went to Pennsylvania's Carlisle Indian School with Leah's uncle, William Jones. They were both involved with drama at Carlisle, and when Anna returned home, she collaborated with Roy on the script. Happy Canyon was an attempt to tell the story of the West in part from the Indian point of view. The first section of the show depicts Indian village life prior to contact with Europeans and Euro-Americans.

But how the Indian and cowboy cultures overlap is still a problem in this Western town. In 2001, a revised Happy Canyon was produced. Indians were given more speaking roles and horses to fight back the U.S. cavalry. They even finally won one battle and mounted a surprise attack on some soldiers. The pageant included more historical materials and, most important, scripted a scene depicting the signing of the 1855 treaty at Walla Walla, when the Confederated Tribes won the right to an independent reservation in the Umatilla Valley. But the debates about the pageant did not stop. There were still skeptics, and in both the Indian and white communities, some people were pushing for more change. To some, the tone of the pageant was wrong. The serious historical treatment of tribal loss and pain jarred against the forced humor of saloon scenes and light-hearted pioneer storytelling.

For years Leah had wanted to see the pageant rewritten. The Happy Canyon roles had always seemed "too static a portrayal of Indians. Indians have changed and whites have changed." Her own family had acted in the pageant since the 1940s. But change, when it came, was difficult. Both Indian and white individuals and families in the community had invested in keeping their parts in the play. And Leah worried that Indians would be forever stuck in two-dimensional roles from the past. She believed that "Indian culture is a living culture, not just historic." She worried about how to breathe life into history and not seal off tribal peoples into a dead past.

The rodeo world was still stuck in the Old West and its obsession with a past that breathed show biz instead of life. The need to keep the people coming through the gates only reinforced the reluctance to change. Even more, economic survival seemed to rest on keeping the familiar stereotypes alive. The moneyed sounds of casino slots and the economic independence of the tribes had not yet cut through the old formulas. Leah and I drank our coffee and talked about the challenges ahead for the tribes trying to shape their future while holding close to their tribal past, not the fantasy of frenzied sideshows.

After our lunch was finished that day, Leah invited me back to her house to continue talking. I followed her gridlike map to her home on the reservation and pulled up in front of a modest, squared-off bungalow, surrounded by flat fields of sage and brush. Leah invited me in and showed me her refrigerator photo gallery covered with snapshots of children and grandchildren. We both laughed about husbands, lovers, and growing old. We spent the rest of the day in her living room, looking through a pile of scrapbooks on the coffee table.

I opened the brittle pages carefully. The first photograph was of Leah and her sister, Etta, who also participated in the Pendleton Round-Up, riding their horses in the "Squaw Race," Thursday, September 13, 1951. The women literally flew across the page, their horses lean and quick, their bodies braced for the run. Leah told me that she would lose five pounds during the roundup. She would get up early, take care of her horse, do the races, ride in the parade, and then sometimes have more races—a "grueling schedule." The races had given Leah and her sister a competitive edge. Their roles in the rodeo were not merely decorative.

A few months earlier, some men involved with the roundup since the 1930s had met me at the Pendleton Round-Up Hall of Fame and told me that the Indian women could ride like the wind. They suspected many Indian women did not want to ride in the Grand Entry today because they would not risk having their traditional buckskin dresses—family heirlooms—damaged in an accident. But they remembered how the Indian women had shone on their horses. Some men even wanted the original Indian races back and the old structure of the Pendleton Round-Up to return, complete with stagecoach racing, trick riding, and roping.

The Pendleton Round-Up was quite progressive in one way: Both Indian and white women were given important symbolic roles in the first half of the century. At Pendleton, Indian women from the Confederated Tribes of the Umatilla Indian Reservation were elected queens in 1926, 1932, 1948, 1952, and 1953. Up to 1953, there were five all-Indian royalty courts representing the roundup, but after that, none. Starting in 1923 and continuing up to the present, Pendleton was also associated with an American Indian Beauty Contest. Before 1952, three of the Indian women winning the beauty contest went on to become queen of the Pendleton Round-Up.

After the mid-1950s, the roles for women at the Pendleton Round-Up became racially divided. Rodeo royalty were white cowgirls, and Indian princesses were Indian princesses, though I have been told that two young Indian women crossed over and became roundup rodeo court princesses.

The history of the Pendleton Round-Up illustrates the shifts in status that rodeo women went through. In the 1910s, the roundup introduced rodeo queens from varied backgrounds. In these early years, queens included movie stars such as Mary Duncan and Josie Sedgwick, the famous rodeo cowgirl Mabel Strickland, and daughters of local businessmen and ranchers drawn from both the Indian and white communities. In that period, rodeo queens could also be rodeo cowgirls. They rode trick horses, roped, raced, and competed with bucking horses and bulls. Mabel Strickland was a good example. Queen of the Pendleton Round-Up in 1927, she had petitioned the rodeo board to compete directly with men for the title of all-around rodeo cowboy. She was refused.

Still, rodeo cowgirls like Bertha Blancett and Prairie Rose Henderson competed against each other in sporting events to huge cheering crowds. In the 1920s, rodeos gave top billing to the ladies' bronc riding and racing events. This heyday did not last long. In 1929, Bonnie McCarroll, a bronc rider and the wife of a bulldogger, or steer wrestler, had a bucking horse fall on her and drag her through the dust at the Pendleton Round-Up. She later died of her injuries. The board of directors decided that their rodeo would never again include the ghastly death of a woman. Men could be hurt and even killed; but no woman would be allowed to ride a bucking horse or a bull again.

Other rodeos still drew big crowds with women bronc riders, but by the late 1940s, women were largely relegated to positions as promoters, that is, rodeo queens. Mary Lou LeCompte, a historian of women in rodeo, claims that Gene Autry's Flying A Rodeo Company, which started in 1942, blended patriotism and decorative roles for women, gradually pushing women out of the arena as contestants and performers and into parades and promotion. Autry's tremendous influence on the rodeo as a big entertainment business shaped how women could participate, but Autry never worked to exclude women altogether. At the Pendleton Round-Up, Indian and white women still raced and competed as trick riders, but even that perennial crowd pleaser vanished for periods of time.

During the 1930s, women began to have a more defined and re-stricted role at Pendleton. In 1934, rodeo royalty began to perform a special daredevil entry, whipping across the arena and over the ground rails. One step from trick riding, this horse-riding display was more entertainment than competition. Rodeo queens could still participate in the competitive races at the roundup if they wanted to, but most stuck to the flashy promotional duties. Over time, both Indian and white women became symbols of the rodeo rather than actors in the arena, competing for money and prizes.

With this history in mind, I asked Leah if she would ever call herself a "cowgirl." "No, definitely not," she answered. She was "Queen of the Pendleton Round-Up." In fact, Leah was one of the last Indian queens for almost a half century. After World War II, when women no longer competed in the arena but rather sold the rodeo, their ethnic background and race became more significant. The rodeo was laced increasingly with patriotism, and its queen was under strong pressure to look and act a particular way. White middle-class women were judged by rodeo boards as the best bet to promote the show.

So why was Leah chosen queen? Leah got involved in the roundup when her mother called her at Willamette University's Lausanne Hall and urged her to come home for tryouts. Looking back, Leah feels that she was selected by the rodeo committee be-cause she was "the Indian in college." As an educated Indian woman, she was safe to represent and promote the rodeo for the committee. She was respectable and middle class.

Leah started her college education at Willamette and then trans-ferred in her junior year to the University of New Mexico. She took drawing and worked in the cafeteria next to Scott Momaday, the writer of *House Made of Dawn*. She talked about her "hidden life" as an artist, how she hitchhiked with her roommates to Jemez pueblo where "art was alive." She learned modern dance and Martha Graham technique from a teacher at the University of New Mexico who had gone to New York and studied with Graham. Years later, after Leah finished her undergraduate degree and her master's in education, she returned to the arts, earning a bachelor's degree in fine arts from the University of Washington in 1980.

Leah's life as an artist was subsumed by the demands of real life—schoolteaching, driving a truck for harvest, and working in libraries and for the reservation. She mentions that Indians have a long history of working as agricultural laborers in the Pacific Northwest. As early as the nineteenth century, they were persuaded or coerced into becoming hired hands for local missionaries.

Leah's story reminds me of Mourning Dove, or Hum-ishu-ma, an Okanogan Indian woman and author of *Cogewea*, a novel published in 1927. Mourning Dove worked the apple harvest in Washington state. She brought along her typewriter, writing in the makeshift tents of migrant workers. Her main character, Cogewea, a young woman of both Indian and white ancestry, rode in the local rodeo and entered both the "ladies" race and the "squaw" race. After she won both races, the judges ruled that only a white woman could win the ladies' race. Her Indian competitors also objected when she tried to claim the "squaw" prize.

I kept paging through Leah's scrapbooks as we talked. In one section was a series of newspaper promotional shots of Leah in 1952: Leah in traditional buckskin dress, Leah in a formal evening gown, Leah in a tennis outfit with tennis racket, Leah with her horse, Leah with a Mixmaster in a kitchen behind a bowl of huckleberries. Leah told me her family teased her mercilessly about this last picture. She was not known as the best huckleberry picker. An important traditional food for many Northwest Indians, huckleberries are still gathered seasonally today. The picture of Leah next to a bowl, stacked high with a shiny mass of berries in an immaculately clean kitchen, still made her laugh. She looked like an Indian June Cleaver.

Her scrapbook contained an editorial titled "An All-American Court," written by one of her mother's friends. The essay criticized the label "All-Indian Court," as if Indians were not Americans. There were pictures of Leah with W. Averell Harriman, with Oregon representatives to Congress, with a New York businessman, a local millionaire, and Oregon governor James Douglas McKay. She showed me a picture of herself with President Harry Truman, presenting him with a Pendleton blanket. When I asked her what that was like, she told me she had been afraid. "Afraid?" I asked. "Of what?" "Well, it was my short hair," Leah replied. She loved her stylish bob, a classy hairdo that she had acquired after her reign as rodeo queen. When she met Truman, she was afraid "her braids would fall off." Now it was my turn to laugh. Of course I knew Leah's hair was cut in a bob from her pictures with family and friends, but in looking at this picture of her in her buckskin dress and braids, I had not noticed the fake hair, worn for the pleasure of the president. It had seemed so "natural."

Sitting in the kitchen of my elderly parents several months after I talked with Leah, I looked through a stack of slides my father had carefully saved from our years as a family in the 1950s. I kept coming back to one picture.

Taken in 1954, a young Indian girl about eight years old stands in front of Mount Rushmore. The four presidents' faces push out of the sparkling white mountain as if they're about to give a speech to the clouds. Dressed in a brilliant turquoise-blue buckskin dress, her black hair braided and tied with vibrant pink pompoms, the young girl looks into the camera without a smile. Thomas Jefferson stares over her shoulder.

I remembered her father talking with my father, telling him how much it would cost to take the picture of the little Indian princess. My father took the photograph and handed the man money. I only knew the girl through this photograph. She was about my age at the time. Long before we saw each other on that day, my culture had invented our strange and strained contact.

For hundreds of years, whites have been spectators of Indian culture and have sometimes paid for the right to watch. They have never tired of ogling traditionally dressed Indians, even while they have actively participated in destroying the economy and cultures of their Indian neighbors. Fragmented and forced identities filter through these exchanges.

An Indian photographer, Zig Jackson, has a series of photographs that depict white tourists taking pictures of Indians in traditional dress dancing at a powwow. A dizzying cultural merry-go-round. To rid themselves of this problem, some Indian reservations have simply outlawed any taking of photographs. How do you reverse hundreds of years of spectatorship? Some Indian photographers like Jackson have suggested and practiced "shooting back," reclaiming photography as a form of artistic expression and social protest. Others have tried to crack open the tired clichés of so-called realistic Indian portraiture and have taken to experimenting with digital images that juxtapose fantasy and reality.

In the early nineteenth century, Indians and whites in the Pacific Northwest came together at Fourth of July celebrations, where they indulged in horse races, gambling, and parades. Alvin Josephy, Jr. writes about how at early nineteenth-century rendezvous with white traders, Nez Perce and Flatheads would perform "equestrian stunts for pay," sell their horses, and trade for firearms and household goods. These gatherings continued for decades. They raised concern among missionaries, who actively tried to suppress these meetings, fearing the Indians were practicing their own culture rather than assimilating and adopting Christianity. This conflict between missionaries and Indians over culture reached levels of farce in the 1890s, when some Presbyterian missionaries living in Kamiah and in Lapwai tried to ban the local Fourth of July celebrations. While most of the missionaries gathered in their homes to fume about the noise outside, two of their brethren slipped outside to watch. They could not resist the urge to see Indians dressed up in their best and performing on horseback.

Alvin Josephy discusses further how the Nez Perce and other Indians in the Northwest used their ceremonial dress and horsemanship to showcase their dignity and strength to the U.S. cavalry. The Indians would ride their horses with daring and skill in thunderous displays, demonstrating to outsiders the collective power of the tribe. As Josephy puts it, the horseback performances were both an honorable salute to guests and a cultural form of resistance. They stated that the Indians were "strong and unafraid, and expected to be treated as a powerful people."

The beauty and pageantry of these displays entranced soldiers and politicians. Some dismissed them as "gaudy" and "heathenish," but more were mesmerized. The whites may have wrenched their treaties from these tribes, but they never recovered from the need to watch and admire them. Spectacles are, after all, ways to look, admire, and indulge a thirst for curiosity as well as a means to humiliate. Ridicule and wonder are combined in the act of looking.

L. G. Moses writes that almost as soon as Europeans saw the cultures of native peoples in the Western Hemisphere, they developed a desire to exhibit these cultures, to place them in the realm of the spectacle. They shipped their native booty back to the courts and the streets of Europe. In 1837, entrepreneur George Catlin, known for his sketches of North American Indian life, opened an Indian gallery in New York City, displaying paintings, artifacts, and reproductions of Indian dwellings. He also brought Indians to London, where they performed scenes for Catlin's vision of Western life. Other entrepreneurs followed with more profit and drive. Arthur Rankin, Dr. N. T. Oliver, and then Buffalo Bill Cody fed off of the hunger of whites to watch warrior dances, Indian drumming, and breakneck horse riding.

Between 1900 and 1917, Wild West shows boomed. Paul Reddin claims that entire towns would shut down when a Wild West show rolled into town. To the tunes of cowboy bands, the epic life on the Plains frontier was depicted in blazing action with chase scenes, duels, and shoot-outs. Violence and the noise of gunpowder punctuated scenes of conflict between Indians and frontiersmen. In Zack Miller's show, an entire act was given over to "Indian Ceremonies and Prairie Pastimes." At the end of the pageant, white settlers fought back the Indians and pushed them off the land.

Why do whites watch? For some whites, the Indian shows were a chance to ridicule a dying and decadent culture. At the 1893 Chicago World's Fair, the ethnographic exhibitions on the midway were an opportunity for white people to gawk at and insult Indians. But for others, Indian spectacles bred a sense of loss and nostalgia, a realization of how quickly cultures lose their bearings. In her novel about her father, *Old Jules*, Mari Sandoz describes a Fourth of July celebration in turn-of-the-century Nebraska. The Indian dancers leapt and chanted, drummed and sang, but the overall effect was "lifeless." The "essence" and "religious significance" of the celebration had vanished. The dance was "debased for a white man's holiday."

The history of how Indians have used whites' desire to watch could occupy an entire chapter, discussing how people resist and adapt to the pressure of conquest. Some Indians, like the man my father met at Mount Rushmore, might have been small-scale entrepreneurs, dressing up their daughters for small change. If whites wanted to watch, then make them pay. No more free gawking. This man may have been furious at having to pander to whites and subject his daughter to a tourist's gaze, turning her into a souvenir or ethnic trophy. His minibusiness could have been an act of despair or an act of defiance, or both. And maybe it was none of the above. That is the problem with my father's photograph: The players are silent.

We don't know who this man and his daughter are, or their personal histories, or what brought them to become souvenirs at Mount Rushmore, so the photograph lends itself to fun-house speculation. All we do know is that the man taking the photograph, my father, had a camera, was a tourist, and collected images, though usually not of Indian people. He preferred sublime landscapes and intimate shots of family members wading in cold mountain streams. But he and I were part of a social story in the 1950s in which white middle-class families began another version of the grand tour, setting out in their automobiles on their summer vacations to travel the newly built interstate and motel system to explore the American West. We were another wave of westward-bound travelers who had already been fed on a steady diet of movie Westerns and would soon be inundated with dozens of prime-time TV shows, all packed with Indians in ceremonial dress, killing white settlers and forming alliances with marginal whites—masked strangers, who watch on tragically as they die. We do know that by the time the photograph was taken in 1954, Indians for hundreds of years had performed for whites and learned how to gain by the exchange and how to keep track of the losses.

Leah's father, Gilbert Conner, grew up amid these cultural tensions. Fluent in several Native American languages and a partial descendent of James Conner, an early mountain man, Gilbert Conner was a member of the Screen Actor's Guild in the early 1950s and had speaking parts in at least two Universal-International movies, *The Great Sioux Uprising* and *Pillars of the Sky*. He enjoyed the movie roles. Parts of *The Great Sioux Uprising* were filmed at Emigrant Hill, very close to where the Wildhorse Gaming Casino stands, which, of course, is nowhere near Sioux country. John War Eagle, a famous Indian actor in the 1950s known for his roles in *Broken Arrow, Pony Soldier, The Great Sioux Uprising,* and *Tonka,* once visited Leah's family and complimented her mother's traditional native cooking. In 1972, he appeared in *When the Legends Die,* the story of an Indian rodeo cowboy.

Since the 1920s, the Pendleton Round-Up has been closely connected with the rise of the Western movie genre. Mabel Strickland, who was rodeo queen of the Pendleton Round-Up in 1927 and previously a championship rodeo cowgirl, was also a movie star, trickrider, and stunt rider. In 1928, Mary Duncan, a movie star from Hollywood, was rodeo queen. At the time, she was starring in the film *Golden Harvest,* filmed in the Pendleton area. Earlier, in 1924, Josie Sedgwick, sister of the film director Edward Sedgwick, had been rodeo queen and had roles in movies such as *Hell's End, The Man Above the Law,* and *The She Wolf.*

The popularity of the Western movie surprised Hollywood. Producers were amazed that American audiences would watch such inexpensively produced flicks. Footage of chase scenes over Western landscapes were recycled and spliced together without much thought because the quality and realism of the scenes really didn't matter. Westerns sold like hotcakes. Leah grew up very aware of this genre. Many Indians are attuned to how their image was manipulated and exploited by popular culture. The question was how to work within this labyrinth of stereotypes and conventions. Where did you begin to perform who you are? Or would that never happen?

By the 1920s, the image of the Indian princess, like its counterpart, the Indian warrior, was entrenched. It had been popular with white audiences for decades, having been widely disseminated on picture postcards and in fiction, epic poetry, Wild West shows, and movies. Some critics argue that the story of the first Indian princess, Pocahontas, had played into a destructive and exploitative American myth of conquest since the colonial period. According to folklore, the erotic and beautiful Pocahontas, the young daughter of Powhatan, a chief of the Algonquian Indians, fell in love with a colonizer, Captain John Smith, and rescued him from certain death in colonial Virginia. Her actions prevented the demise of the white settlers. Aside from the fact that Pocahontas was probably a little girl when she met Smith, the story also omits her kidnapping and rape by the English, her conversion to Christianity before marrying John Rolfe, a tobacco planter, her voyage to London in 1616, and her death at the age of twenty-two. Pocahontas is buried in a churchyard at Gravesend, England.

Even today, popular culture industries like Walt Disney Productions continue to make Indian women objects of erotic fantasy. Disney's animated version of the Pocahontas story does feature the violence and greed of British settlers and offers Pocahontas a few speeches about keeping the land green. But Pocahontas is a curvaceous babe whose destiny is to fall in love with a white man. The film critic Jacquelyn Kilpatrick noted that Glen Keane, the key animator of the film, researched historical images of Pocahontas but dropped them for a bombshell with Asian eyes and ample breasts.

In 1926, when Esther Motanic became Pendleton's rodeo queen, the image of Indian women as princess was formulaic. The honorary Indian princesses were selected by the tribes, who insisted they were deserving of respect, but the princesses were required to wear traditional Indian regalia, displaying exotic beauty for a white audience. Again, I think of Mourning Dove in the 1920s, who posed for her book-cover photograph in buckskin and beads. Later, in an act of resistance, she asked to have a picture of her taken with her car. She refused to become a museum piece. She left the conventional image of Pocahontas behind.

What happens, however, when an Indian woman becomes the queen of the roundup and represents both the white and Indian community? What are the implications when she accepts the role of representing the entire community across the racial divide and is no longer limited to the title of honorary Indian princess? Does she become a voice of resistance? Or a voice of assimilation? Can her regalia then become a constant reference point, almost a weaving, of her family and community history, acting as a memorial of the past with the power to represent a complex historical and political world? When Leah was queen, she wore both traditional Indian outfits and modern Western dress. She moved across the fixed costumes of different identities.

At her home, Leah asked me to watch clips from a video produced by the Oregon Historical Society and the Oregon Trail Coordinating Council. As a tribal elder, she narrated family and tribal stories about the Oregon Trail. The first clip showed Leah telling a story handed down in her family that expressed sorrow for the white settlers traveling on the trail. The overlanders' children looked exhausted and wore no shoes. The adults were disheveled. Leah's ancestors felt sympathy for their plight. Later, when speaking about the Oregon Trail, she referred to it as "still zooming past us. It's Interstate 84 now."

Without Leah's voice, the video would reinforce the sense of the Oregon Trail as a relic from a vanished past that must be preserved with interstate markers, interpretive centers, and guided tours, a past available only through tourism and scenic turnoffs from the highway. Her voice makes it clear that the past lives today; it has only transformed its shape.

Toward the end of my visit at her home, Leah told me that after she was queen of the Pendleton Round-Up she went to one of the early All-American Indian Days held in Sheridan, Wyoming, in 1953. She went through the tryouts for the second annual Miss Indian American Pageant. She saw the Indian pageant as a response to the Miss America Pageant that was sweeping the media by storm in the 1950s. Creating a model of beauty based on whiteness, the Miss America Pageant went on for decades as a monoracial event.

Leah went to the Miss Indian American Pageant with a group of five or six women from Pendleton, including her younger sister, Etta, who was a runner-up in the pageant. At the pageant, she met Indians from all over the United States—Navajos, Crows, and Cheyennes. She felt the power of Indian cultures other than her own. For the first time, she came to understand the Sun Dance and the strange beauty of Cheyenne music. She was awed by the entrance of 300 Crow dancers and wondered how the emigrants must have felt when they heard the singing and chanting of the Crows for the first time. The women who were chosen to be on the court of Miss Indian America went on to leadership positions in their tribes and were professionally successful outside the tribe. Leah wanted me to understand that beauty was not merely a function of physical image but was connected to moral strength and political leadership for women.

Events like the Miss Indian America Pageant and the All-American Indian Days were opportunities for Indian peoples to represent themselves in the symbolic landscape of America, and not merely in the convenient stereotyped minority roles so popular in the movies and radio shows of the 1950s. Leah also felt that they were a precursor to the successful powwow circuit of the 1990s, the next stage in intertribal gatherings where dance, feasting, and festivities crossed over a range of Indian cultures throughout the United States.

The struggle over culture by Indian peoples is by no means finished. In fact, for Leah it has barely begun. For centuries, whites have acted as spectators, producers, and directors of Indian culture. It was not until the 1980s that the Smithsonian Institution finally appointed an Indian, Richard West, Jr., to be the curator of its Indian collections. This legacy has left a hunger in the hearts of many Indians to control the representation of their culture. Only then could their past be redressed, rewritten, and reclaimed.

For Leah, the rodeo has ceased as a place where Indians can find that control. For her, Indians live in a world next to the rodeo, where they are developing creative possibilities of cultural exchange, a world in which they have more power over how culture is made, reproduced, and distributed. One in which they have the capital to build their own museums and art galleries like the Tamástslikt Cultural Institute next to the Wildhorse Gaming Resort on the Umatilla Indian Reservation. Today, Leah puts her energy into working with the Tiimutla Art Council, organizing shows and exhibitions to promote the arts, not the rodeo, on the reservation.

I left her home, realizing that for Leah the roundup had long ceased to celebrate the local community. As a cultural ritual and now a professional sport, it habitually told only one story, flattening out the past and the differences between the people who lived and worked next to each other. I was left wondering how the nation as a whole could reimagine how to celebrate together. Could we breathe new life into old forms, or must we invent entirely new ones in which the old roles dissolve and slip away and the old hungers for spectacle are replaced by participation and exchange?

6

Queen for a Day

Flattened wheat fields spread out for miles around Jean's ranch house in central Washington. Close by, enormous skeletal caterpillars with twin-wheeled feet stretch irrigation pipes across thirsty crops. Their noonday mist creates dozens of repeated rainbows in the harsh light. Jean has always been surrounded by wheat. Her father had farmed in northern Idaho and her mother's family had homesteaded there in the 1870s. Jean grew up in a farming family. Her mother canned everything they ate, filling the kitchen pantry with mason jars of beans, peaches, and pickles. There was a weariness in Jean's voice when she talked about the work. The stillness in the house only made it seem more oppressive.

In 1954, Jean was rodeo queen of the Lewiston Roundup. "It was a lovely experience," she said settling into her couch in a large living room with a huge picture window opening onto a still October sky. Everything about Jean and her house was quiet. I was tempted to fill in the moments of silence until I realized the stillness was part of the conversation. Instead, I would smooth out my notepad, or fuss with my tape recorder, or merely wait.

Jean was deliberate. Her hands were carefully folded on her lap. She took time to tell me about what it was like to grow up a farm girl in the late 1940s and early 1950s. What it was like to be chosen rodeo queen. What it was like to wonder how her life could have been different. She loved books and had wanted to be a librarian, but that dream would have to wait for another lifetime.

As a child, she had escaped the hard work of the farm by catching the Westerns at matinees in town. The Westerns were all about Roy. By 1942, Roy Rogers had surpassed Gene Autry as the "King of the Cowboys." He and his horse, Trigger, and his wife, Dale Evans, and his sidekick, Gabby Hayes, brought in big crowds across the United States. Jean liked him even better than Dale.

Growing up, Jean did not have a television. She would have to wait until college to catch *The Roy Rogers Show*. In the 1950s, television Westerns such as *Gunsmoke, Rawhide, The Rifleman, Have Gun, Will Travel,* and *Maverick* became household entertainment. By 1959, forty-eight different Westerns had been produced for prime-time television. The boom of TV Westerns lasted until the early 1960s, capturing more than one-third of the viewing audience, and Westerns remained top-rated shows until the early 1970s. Without the television Western, Jean idolized the new heroes of the silver screen. Cowboys and cowgirls had a glow about them. They were celebrities. Rodeo queens shared that glow. They made you "starry-eyed."

Starry-eyed—a new word slipped into my conversations with women who were rodeo queens in the 1950s. Their selection as queen was not a surprise, a quirk, or a sudden change of status; it was a fantasy just within reach, encouraged by their communities, fed by popular culture, and enjoyed with the reckless longing of youth. They were mesmerized by the rodeo queens who visited their grade schools, rode in their hometown parades, and sometimes made appearances with Western movie stars like Slim Pickens or Walter Brennan. They wanted to have the eyes that gazed out strongly from beneath the sexy curved cowboy hat. They wanted to ride the palomino horse just like Trigger and wear the soft buckskin gloves. They wanted to be cowgirl celebrities.

Daydreaming on their front porches and lying awake at night, they turned the popcorn fantasy over in their minds. They imagined themselves action heroes, the wonder women of a new age. But they had to be careful. The 1950s also urged them to follow Mrs. Cleaver into the kitchen. It fed them images of innocent longing and ferocious, yet fragile, female sexuality, complete with pillbox hats and pointed bras. Doris Day waltzed next to Marilyn Monroe and Lana Turner. Jean knew the contradiction only too well. Its consequences still affected her life.

For my visit, I had brought along several old photographs I had found of Jean in the photography morgue of a local newspaper. I placed the first one on the coffee table between us and asked her what she thought about the picture. Could she remember how she felt when it was taken? She glanced at the photo and looked away. Her gentle voice hesitated; a look of sadness crept into her eyes. Taken in 1954, the black-and-white photo showed her dressed and posed as an *Annie Get Your Gun* walk-on. Legs spread wide, arms on her hips, she looked aslant at the camera and flirted, her thick lipstick painting a coy smile. We looked silently at the photo. I was reluctant to ask her again about the pose, afraid I was bringing up memories best left alone. She finally spoke with hardly any expression. "I suppose I was supposed to look sexy there, huh? I don't know. I don't know what he had in mind. I suppose I just did what he told me to. They just told me what to do and I did it." A touch of resignation and resistance strained her voice. She seemed to regret how pliable she had been in the photographer's hands.

Her subdued reply contrasted sharply with the image of the perky young woman in the photo who looked like she might burst into song at any moment: "Anything you can do, I can do better. I can do anything better than you." Hitting the stage right after World War II, *Annie Get Your Gun* had sung its way into the hearts of Americans, with a film version in 1950, a TV series, *Annie Oakley,* in 1952, and numerous stage revivals.

Lyricist Dorothy Fields, who created Annie's words, sensed that the time was right for a strong woman character who could compete directly against men and win. Annie is both a sweetheart and a gun-toting, hardheaded sharpshooter. But as we all know, when her skill with guns threatens to destroy her success at romance, she gives up her quest for glory to marry the man. Sociologists have long discussed the endemic problem of women's fear of success, as if there were some invisible rule according to which women lose their femininity if they compete too well against men. Losing femininity means losing big. No love, no husband, no family. In the 1950s, a woman without the love of a man was an outcast.

The real Annie Oakley always wore skirts and presented herself as a lady, though she occasionally dressed up as an Indian princess. She was no Calamity Jane, who wore men's clothing and posed with her gun, having lost the desire or need to curl her hair, paint her face, or otherwise display her femininity. On Broadway, Annie was more a blend of the historical Annie and Calamity Jane. She adopted a working-class voice and rough manners.

Jean was not impressed by the photograph. She loved the rodeo queen outfit she wore in the picture, but the pose was not the way she felt about herself. "Sexy" was the photographer's fantasy. Jean remembered feeling classy and admired, dressed up in her rodeo queen outfit. The rodeo board didn't want you "in your blue jeans" or "hobnobbing in the barns in your beautiful white suit."

I had another photograph of Jean that I had spent time thinking about before my visit. Jean is posed in a kitchen, leaning on a counter, staring at a glass, as if she's trying to figure out if it's bright and sparkling enough for the spot-free 1950s. The white enamel kitchen is like a stage set, revealing the frustrated, perturbed housewife. She scowls at the glass as if it were an enemy. I could imagine her tossing it on the floor the second after the picture was taken.

Jean looked at the photograph and laughed. "These were girl things I had to do and I really didn't want to do them. Here I am having to dry dishes and I really don't want to. I'd rather be off with my friend riding horses than doing my mother's dishes. We didn't have a dishwasher then, either." Jean saw the anger and resistance in the picture. When she was young, she always tried to get out of the kitchen.

These two photos captured for me the strange social landscape white women entered after World War II. They had to be sexy, and they became sexy with their wonder bras, reinforced girdles, and clinging knit dresses and sweater tops, but they also had to be domestic, clutching irons and draped in housedresses. They could possess some of the powerful tools white men had at their disposal—education, money, and prestige—but they could only have access to these new powers if they behaved like ladies.

During our day together, Jean talked about how a lady could be sexy, but not athletic. Athleticism edged a woman up close to male strength. There were limits to how much Jean was allowed to develop her expertise with horses, for example. As a young woman, she was discouraged from developing "ugly muscles." She lived with this warning about having her beauty dissolve along with her ability to attract a man if her body grew too strong.

She rode her horse anyway. She wanted to escape the world of housekeeping and explore the outdoors. "What time I could escape, yes, that was my time. I'd go off with a friend and spend a whole day and come back in time to help with supper. Sometimes we got into mischief." The wheat hills drew her constantly away from her predictable future.

She also felt that rodeo queens were a Western elite, polished and well-mannered, not tough old cowgirls or wild women who stayed out on their horses too long and too late. Another queen from the 1950s whom I interviewed fondly remembered a girl-friend who grew up on a ranch, cursed, drank, and thought rodeo queens a bunch of sissies. She laughed hard about her friend's blunt indiscretions but admitted how important it was to her in the 1950s to be called a lady by her family and boyfriends.

Jean replied emphatically that in the 1950s, "if you behaved, you had guaranteed respect." The rules were pretty clear for a rodeo queen. "I was sitting there like a figurehead in my beautiful uni-form and my beautiful shoes and my beautiful hat, saying 'Good morning, sir. How do you do?'" At rodeo time, her role as queen had mandated restraints. She was "allowed to run little calves out of the arena when they were calf roping and that was it. Very lim-ited. I certainly wasn't out there riding the bulls out. And the rest of the time you put your horse away and you went and sat in your box." A lady in a box—Jean chafed at the memories. You could be Annie, but then you had to give up being Annie. In the end, her world hated ambiguity. Men were men, and ladies, well, were ladies. Her "wonderful summer" as a rodeo queen in 1952 let her live outside the box, but then returned her to its stationary walls. "We were just stuck. I could be a teacher, I could be a nurse, I could be a secretary and that was just about it. You were expected to get married and have two kids and raise your children."

How different Jean's story was from that of Mardell, a rodeo queen in 1947, who had found the war years a great chance to up-set gender roles. Because all the young men were gone, she could act out her dreams. She lived in a lookout, watching for fires in a National Forest, and was accepted into veterinary school. She went on to become the first woman veterinarian in Montana. She was lucky. After the war, women were no longer accepted in vet school. The window closed. Eventually, Mardell stopped working to raise a family, but in the 1970s, she returned to the work she had been trained to do.

Born seven years after Mardell, Jean felt she never had the choice. The 1950s script was too powerful. Its hold was still in effect. Even though Jean criticized the role of lady, she wouldn't let it go. She worried about "civility" among young people today. "I find the younger generation to be growing up without manners. There's a rudeness out there somewhere that I don't like. That wasn't there in the Fifties." If you didn't behave properly when she was young, you didn't receive respect. And without respect, women were in danger. How men and women treated each other was important for Jean. How would women gain respect if they abandoned the old ways that guaranteed them certain treatment by men? The rodeo queen in the 1950s was a limited lady, but she received all the benefits the role delivered. What would take its place? In a world without ladies, men were predators without social restraint.

Even rodeo reflected these changes to her. In the 1990s, the rodeo had become a blood sport with the recent surge of interest in all-bull rodeos. "People are coming to see violence. I find that a little scary. . . . You might just cheer if some old cowboy got stomped . . . Then you are going back to Roman times and you might as well put a lion and a Christian in there." She had even drifted away from the old rodeo world she knew growing up. Like Blanche, she did not like the use of the flank strap on bucking horses. She preferred to go to draft-horse shows. She wanted to see how the rider and horse interacted and worked together to pull a load or select out cows. She did not want to see blood.

Before I left, Jean showed me her rodeo queen outfit. She had draped the shiny white blouse and pants over a chair and had placed the polished white boots beneath the hanging pant legs. The empty outfit drooped in the chair like a wilted flower. "It's beautiful," I said. "Yes," Jean sighed. She drew her hands lightly over the embroidery on the blouse. "It was a lovely experience. People were nice to me, though I expected them to be. Women and men were very gracious and kind to me."

I drove home thinking about another photograph I had found in the photography morgue. It showed a picture of a 1952 *Queen for a Day* winner visiting the Lewiston Roundup with her husband. The Queen for a Day was the winner of a game show that started on radio in 1945 and was then transformed for TV. Female contestants had to tell a story. The sob story that received the most support or sympathy from the audience, based on audience applause, won. The applause level was measured by a machine whose dial registered sound volume. Competing against the other contestants for collective tears, only one woman went on to become "Queen for a Day," a sudden and temporary celebrity. In this daytime psychodrama, the anonymous housewife could find instant fame. Women ironed at home in front of the television and cried along.

In the photo, the Queen for a Day is beaming for the camera while her husband holds a bouquet of flowers. Two rodeo queens stand in the background talking. The roles are neatly divided. Clutching her purse and husband, one woman must make you cry; decked out in buckskin fringe, cowboy hat, and pants, the other two must take your breath away. Both had to conform to the rules, whether to garner sympathy or generate applause. Domestic or wild, both had to behave like perfect ladies.

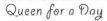

I didn't have a chance to meet Susan face-to-face. She lived too far away, but we talked for hours on the phone. I had found several photographs of her when she was a young rodeo queen. A striking brunette with short curly hair, she was dressed in one shot in an embroidered, pleated sundress, sitting in the shadows of her porch, writing in her notebook. Through the speakerphone, her energized voice filled the small conference room where I had spread out my notebooks on a long narrow table. Her long rolls of heartfelt laughter bounced off the walls. Susan was living in southern California and had long since left the rural West behind, but not before she had competed for rodeo queen titles at the local, regional, state, and national levels. The 1950s of her youth was lived among a Western elite brimming with playful duplicity.

Queens in the 1950s were often daughters of rodeo board members, who in turn were the department store, car dealership, or successful ranch owners. To Susan, these men, who wanted their wives and daughters to be ladies, were also the men who liked to play cowboy, demanded games of amusement, and thought drinking and whoring would get them closer to their ideal of masculinity. They cheated on their wives and thrived on fantasies about the West. They had bought it and now they owned it. With emphasis, Susan said, "It was the old West fantasy—the macho men ride horses, the cowboy thing." Imitating the voice of her father's generation, she strutted the words, "We put on our cowboy hat and our boots and our string ties and we swagger for a couple of weeks and we are big deals." They were living the myth and loved it.

Her description sounded similar to that of the writer Jack Kerouac, who wandered the American highways in the 1950s. In his classic autobiographical novel, *On the Road*, the main character, Sal Paradise, made no attempt to hide his disappointment at what he discovered in Cheyenne, Wyoming. At Wild West Week, the real West had disappeared beneath a stifling world of make-believe. "Fat businessmen in boots and ten-gallon hats" stroll through Oldtown with "their hefty wives in cowgirl attires." Paradise reacted with disgust; the display was ridiculous. In his "first shot at the West," he had witnessed "to what absurd devices it had fallen to keep its proud tradition." The West had become a costume ball created and attended by the middle classes for their amusement.

Kerouac's disillusionment went hand in hand with his idealization of the West and its "proud tradition." His disappointment became part of a language of disenchantment found everywhere on writings about the American West. Kerouac did not question whether the noble past ever existed. He acted as if it had, absolutely. He imagined the West as a lost golden age, wounding the present with its impossible reminders.

Disenchantment encouraged many people to damn what they considered inauthentic in the West. Cowboys and cowgirls, whether in the rodeo or on the ranch, were constantly evaluated against these fanciful demands of a mythical golden age existing sometime in the nineteenth century. Rodeo queens had to justify themselves in some way as the real thing with real roots in the real American West or they were shunted aside.

The first and only time I called what the rodeo queens wore "costumes," I was reprimanded by two rodeo queen chaperones. Never, ever say "costumes." In the rodeo world, queens wore "outfits." "Costumes" imply the theatrical and make-believe. Such associations are forbidden. In a way, the rodeo West had become an immense nostalgia machine, reproducing claims about authenticity and moaning on about disenchantment at the same time. In the 1950s, the rodeo queen was already propping up the farce.

A few of the rodeo queens I interviewed startled me with their frankness about the sham of the rodeo. Susan was one. When I asked her what the rodeo had to do with everyday life in the West, this rodeo queen said, "Everything." Although they weren't raised on ranches, her father's generation adopted cowboy ways. Privileged, they could play with these images like other people played with clothes. Susan's father was a successful businessman in town, but he cultivated a rural lifestyle that brought drama and excitement to her family. "My Dad was what you would call a 'gentleman rancher.' We had a small herd of cattle that we did not run on our property. We ran up around Fernwood, Idaho. Ranching was mostly for pleasure." With ranching for pleasure came an interest in the rodeo board. "It was very macho to be on the rodeo board. Macho guys were on the rodeo committee. A distinct section of men who were kind of celebrated as men. There were no women on the rodeo board." As a daughter of a rodeo board member, Susan grew up sharing in the fantasy.

"It got to be just an understood thing that the daughters of the board who were any kind of horsewoman at all would eventually try out." Try out she did, and went on to spend a significant part of three years as a rodeo queen. "My father made it for me. But I wanted to do it." When Susan's older friends became queens, nothing could stop her determination to join the charmed circle. Her father's world was a magnet with its bigger-than-life roles for men and women. If men could be "macho," women could be "glamorous."

The strength and power of the rodeo board was connected to the Chamber of Commerce and other civic institutions in the town. They set the tone for the rodeo in the 1950s, turning its social space into a country club atmosphere of parties and wealth. Selected, not elected, the rodeo queen was a symbol of the economic and civic leadership in the community. Throughout the 1950s, the rodeo queen and her court were center stage at local country clubs. Their pressed gabardine suits, spotless hats, and friendly smiles fit in perfectly underneath the wide umbrellas of patio tables where buffet breakfasts were served to the impeccably dressed wives in town.

Susan went on to be Miss Rodeo Idaho and Miss Rodeo America in the late 1950s. As she said, at "eighteen you are pretty convincible." Gary Cooper placed the crown on her head at the Flamingo Hotel in Las Vegas and Robert Horton of the top television series, *Wagon Train,* and Bob Barker of *Truth or Consequences,* who would later direct generations of Miss America contestants through the tension of pageant nerves, presented her with the Miss Rodeo America trophy.

Rodeo queens not only represented the strange mix of wildness and glamour demanded by the rodeo board but, ironically, also helped make rodeo respectable for a middle-class audience. Susan was clear about the role of Miss Rodeo America in the 1950s: She was intended "to change the image of the rodeo by glamorizing it a little bit, getting the emphasis off the pain and suffering of the animal, getting it more recognized as a legitimate sport." Changing the image of the rodeo also meant changing the image of the cowboys.

It was a tough job. After all, the rodeo cowboy was a working-class image and a fantasy of class resistance for the middle-class male. Rodeo queens did not marry rodeo cowboys. They could flirt and fantasize, but their parents and the rodeo boards and organizations did their best to keep queens and cowboys apart. As respectable ladies, the queens were urged to get on with their lives, finish their education, and marry someone who would provide them with security and money.

Susan looked back with humor and irony on the relationship of the rodeo cowboy and the rodeo queen. The rodeo queen was forced into one side of a simple, good girl–bad girl formula. She was the "cold queen" in opposition to the "cowboy slut," the groupies or buckle bunnies who hung around the rodeo cowboys and got drunk on their macho energy.

Like Jean, she insisted, "You had to maintain yourself as a lady." In the highly sexualized world of the rodeo, the queen needed to walk a straight and narrow line. A rodeo cowboy could be her "buddy" or "friend," even take the role of "brother," but that was it. A queen who had a sexual liaison with a cowboy ran the risk of severe reprimand from the rodeo organization and even dismissal. "There was no way that even if I had been madly in love with a cowboy I would have ever gone out publicly, dancing, kissed him, gone to bed with him or whatever. It's a small club. The word would spread like lightning. It was better to be the cold queen than the hot body."

No matter how much the promoters polished the cowboy image, the cowboys remained dangerous coworkers. Susan remembered how selfish her cowboy cohorts were. "They were more concerned about what they were going to do to make show than what their family was doing back wherever they were. Lots of times they just plain outright lied about having a family. They were picking up women in the bars. You saw the sleeping around. You saw the grandiosity. They all are macho, everyone of them. The longer they stayed in it, the more they were inclined."

The rodeo cowboy's values were deceptive and deceiving. He went down the road for his own pleasure and excitement. Girlfriends and wives were left behind to worry and wait, or they had to accommodate themselves to life on the road, sitting in the stands, hoping for the best. There was no consistent income and no security. Men played cowboy because they wanted to get away from the domestic roles of the middle class, and they equated women with the stranglehold of these roles. Whether for two weeks, two years, or a lifetime, they skipped out on their ladies.

Rodeo queens both participated in the glow of this anti-domestic world and enforced its necessary limits.

Susan's laughter was infectious. "Cowboys love to flirt," she snickered. She was a ladylike queen to "make cowboys look like they were not just chasing bimbos. They had such a negative image—drunken crazy people, rough, crude, rude." The Western mystique, whether in rodeo, movies, or television, needed to conform to expectations about middle-class respectability and a new professionalism. Through her glamour and poise, the rodeo queen lent legitimacy to the view of rodeo as a place where serious athletes competed for success. Rodeo queens promoted rodeo as a "true sport where [it took] real talent and real ability to go out there and do what those guys do and risk their lives doing it." Women were not mere frosting on the cake; they were making the cake possible.

As tough as he was, the cowboy had returned to the white middle class with new avenues of expression and acceptance in the 1950s. He had entered the living rooms of America through television, and rodeo tried to ride on the expanding audience. The rodeos of the 1950s were often linked with movie and television celebrities who signed autographs and made appearances. The television promoters saw the rodeo audiences as part of the emerging market of television viewers. The rodeo promoters saw Western movie and television stars as gate getters. The association worked, particularly when more and more middle-class American families like my own took their two-week vacations wandering the new interstate highways crisscrossing the West, living out their fantasies and returning home renewed by a Western adventure.

In the 1950s, rodeo queens entered this national media spotlight. In 1955, a group of businessmen invented the concept of Miss Rodeo America and founded International Rodeo Management to organize, fund, and develop the pageant. In 1958, they

moved the pageant to Las Vegas, where it stayed until 1973. After about ten years in Oklahoma City, the pageant returned to Las Vegas, where it is held today. With the increase in visibility, the responsibilities for the rodeo queens skyrocketed. "You run your butt off. There was a tremendous demand of my time and my energy. People have high expectations of what you should do and be." The pressures could be grueling. "Always smiling, always being in a good mood, always looking beautiful, always looking perfectly groomed. Your boots were clean; your gloves were clean. I spent a lot of time polishing white boots and powdering white hats. And then the expectation of riding into an arena, speed on a horse. We did come in at high speed."

When it came to national competition at the Miss Rodeo America pageant, Susan felt that almost everyone who tried out for the national pageant in the 1950s was an excellent horsewoman. The difference was in the poise and public image the woman could project. The stress of the competition had long-term rewards. Susan knows that her life was helped by her years as rodeo royalty. She learned how to organize her time, how to work with people as varied as rough cowboys and "prissy" ladies, and how to handle herself in public. "I grew up very quickly. For me it had a tremendously positive effect. I was from a very small town. . . . I was no longer a country kid. I had all of a sudden seen the world. I was much better prepared for college than a lot of people who came from the city. I knew how to budget my time. I am the most organized human being. That was all very good training. You don't have a choice. You just do it. It has helped me professionally my whole life, too."

Even though she served as a symbol of her father's fantasies and the rodeo establishment's need to gain respectability, there was space for Susan to gain power through the role of rodeo queen and to use this power to change her life. The strain was worth the effort. It led to renewed commitment. "It really helped me identify the things I really wanted to do with my life." A former teacher, a counselor, and radio-show host, Susan learned flexibility and strength by having to be on display and under pressure. There was a chance to meet people she would never have known, to test herself against the demands and pressures of strangers, and to gain a sense of confidence that has never left her. The benefits were many.

Although rodeo queens would never equate themselves with beauty queens, the parallels are there. After World War II, the Miss America beauty pageant became patriotic, respectable, and profitable. It constructed a national concept of beauty for the middle-class: the tall, sexy white woman. Particular types of bodies, talents, and speaking abilities were rewarded; others were denigrated. The same was true of the Miss Rodeo America contest, which was also the exclusive domain of white women.

Still, there were some major distinctions between the Miss Rodeo America contest and national beauty pageants. By requiring women to be excellent horsewomen with a knowledge of rodeo, the rodeo competition put women in a less conventional gender role. They could wear pants, ride wild, and still be ladies. Their class and style gave them the right to play hard without abandoning the expected roles of middle-class women.

After the 1950s, rodeo queens became public symbols of virginity. Young, beautiful, and potentially the perfect wife and mother, they had to remain virgin queens during their reign. As in other beauty pageants, pregnancy was total anathema to the role. Women violating the code were punished. Gossip floated around about certain rodeo queens, but if they crossed the line, they were gone. I heard stories about queens decades after their indiscretions. No one forgot the pregnancies.

The virgin queens were eroticized. As one rodeo princess from Cheyenne Frontier Days once told me, there is something incredi-

bly sexy about women racing around on their horses at the edge of the arena before the rodeo action begins. The blood boils; the semen moves. Paul Shepard has called horse riding a "love affair going back half a million generations." In human history, both men and women shared in this love affair, yearning for the "Pegasus effect," the desire to enter the sensual, magical, and psychic world of the horse. From the pictographs on cave walls to elaborate oral epics, horses have inhabited the human erotic imagination for thousands of years. In the rodeo, the queen and her princesses evoke the fertile joy of pure motion, electric and unstoppable.

These women differed from their domestic sisters. They were allowed to appropriate some of the masculine power of the rodeo. Even though they play a largely symbolic role in the actual rodeo, they siphoned off some of the attributes of the heroic male cowboy. They dressed in feminized cowboy clothing, they rode with daring and confidence, they enjoyed speed and were not contained within the measured carefulness of the lady's pace. Given this power, they were then asked to wrap it up in the conventions of the lady and to control its possible threat to male power and sexuality. Only then could they become celebrities and receive the applause. Later, in their domestic roles, untouched by the glamour of the rodeo queen, they were left like the Queen for a Day with stories of domestic sorrow, tragedy, and loss—sympathy, not admiration, their reward.

Hidden Horses

It was one of those washed-blue sky days. The clouds were too white. I had to shield my eyes from their brilliance as they rushed above me. The air smelled clean, and its cool taste woke me up. I was to meet Isabel in the pasture to the side of her parent's farmhouse, a sloping home of graying wood. The horses were out back grazing, two mares, one with a foal two days old, the other ready to foal. Partially hidden by the shade of locust trees, the two mares were suspicious of my presence and eyed me from a long way off. Isabel, a spry, thin woman in her sixties, deftly grabbed a metal pail, scooped up some grain from a sack and headed out. She wasn't going to wait all day for them to make up their minds whether to act friendly.

Barely 7 A.M., the sun was starting to warm up the pasture. I could already feel the heat through my heavy jeans. In a few minutes, I could see Isabel leading the mares down away from the trees, waving the pail to entice them into the social world of humans. I started walking toward them, moving slowly so as not to frighten them. I had strayed only a few yards when the foal burst from the tall grass and almost knocked me over. He was full of new life and bounded away like a young deer. As his compact blackness whirled by me, I caught a glimpse of his markings, a white blanket with black spots on his rump, a modernist painting flying through a meadow. He was all go and he knew it.

Isabel came out every morning before work to check on them. She felt she was lucky to have this pasture at the family home to keep them in while the foals grew. She didn't mind the drive or the hour. Many women I know give up nice clothes, better furniture, even cars to keep their horse. They are "horse-poor" and even find themselves unable to pay their monthly bills in order to keep these animals in their daily life. One horse seems to turn into two, then three, maybe even four. Somehow the horse becomes the center of their life. Many a marriage suffers because of this shift in priority.

Near where I live, a woman had brought her beloved horse to a local barn. Her horse had turned mean and was quick to shy and kick. It had a history. The mare had been repeatedly beaten by the woman's husband in their backyard barn. He knew that the most effective way he could hurt his wife was not by slapping her across the face or punching her in the stomach. How much crueler to walk out to their barn and slug her horse with a two-by-four. Trapped in its stall, the horse could never quite evade the blow. The marriage had ended, and the horse was now on a slow road to mending its wounds and relearning to trust human beings. It would take years to undo the beatings. How could a horse make sense of domestic abuse?

Out in the pasture, Isabel looked at ease. She was focused and clear about her movements as she walked toward the foal. Her graying hair flew about the collar of her starched white shirt when she reached for the newborn horse, coaxing the energy burst to accept the touch of her hand. She made sure the mare did not feel threatened and reassured her with her voice. "It's okay." The foal sniffed the air and her scent. He seemed to relax for a moment. Isabel stayed still and the foal approached.

A few days earlier, I had talked with Isabel in her office. She was in high gear, juggling the demands of directing the Upward Bound program at the University of Idaho. She wanted to talk, but the strain was apparent. Students were lined up outside her office, waiting for her time. After some quick conversations with her staff, she managed to close the door. In the quiet, Isabel told me how much she puzzled over the bond between people and horses. Growing up on a farm, she had yearned for a horse as a young girl. Her parents did not have money to waste on a pleasure horse, but when she was nine or ten, her uncle managed by trading to acquire a saddle horse for her and her siblings to ride.

Later, her family became more directly involved with horses when the federal government sponsored a program in the late 1940s to distribute stallions to families and individuals who had the facilities to keep them. "There was an era when the government was interested in a remount program, I believe they called it. And as I understood it, the government placed stallions around with people that were willing to take them for the purpose of generating more riding horses in the area. I believe they referred to these stallions as remount stallions and a program to remount. I would have to assume there was a depletion of the number of horses in the West and an interest in reestablishing a horse population." Isabel's own horse was the offspring of one of these remount stallions.

From 1908 to 1948, the army ran its Remount Service to improve the quality and quantity of their horse and mule stock. Select civilian breeders raised horses in seven distinct regions in the United States, guided by the recommendations and regulations of army officers. About 75 percent of the foals were then purchased by the army. World War I had wreaked havoc on these animals, killing 68,000 as they carried cavalry and supplies into battle. By the late 1940s, the army had little use for horses because jeeps and trucks had become the means for transporting troops and supplies. In 1948, the remount program was transferred to the Department of Agriculture, which quickly stopped the breeding program and disbursed the herds as the development of the railroad and the switch to tractors made horses irrelevant to transportation and agriculture. Horses were no longer needed for war or farming. They were now instruments of pleasure.

Isabel rode bareback for years before the rodeo board came out to her farm to see her ride. "I wasn't the kind of horseback rider who had boots and regalia and hats and so forth. I was just this sort of rider who probably rode 99 percent of the time bareback. I grew up learning to ride bareback. I didn't have a saddle until later when probably I was in high school. I worked for my father in the summer and the payment for working for him in the summer—and I think I drove truck so I was fourteen, fifteen—was this saddle. . . . So I didn't have boots. And I didn't have a hat. So when they came to see me ride, why I was just in a pair of jeans and tennis shoes and a T-shirt, I suppose. I was very surprised and probably unaware of what this was all about. But I was always interested in horses . . . I could have just lived on a horse, day and night."

When I asked her about her year as rodeo princess in 1951, she surprised me by saying she "did not have the aspiration to be on the court." But she did have the drive to work tirelessly with her horse. She would never deny that she had had a wonderful summer as royalty for the Lewiston Roundup. When Isabel rode her horse in the rodeo parades and the arena, she felt like a "dancer putting on a performance at a ballet." Instead of slippers, she had her horse. "I don't think I saw it as being all that daring and maybe I didn't see it as being inappropriate or an unusual role. If anything, I suppose, I saw it as the opportunity to demonstrate something that had been going on all the time and maybe had not had any real appreciation or recognition. . . . To me it was this golden opportunity to demonstrate a skill and a talent that maybe only my immediate family had ever really shown any appreciation for."

The often hidden life of women with horses—the after-school hours, the early mornings, the weekends working in the barn, the long days grooming, washing, and riding—was paid off with recognition and praise. Isabel's skill, knowledge, and strength now had a public face.

The celebrity glow of rodeo royalty was not important to Isabel. What lasted was the way her love of horses connected her to family and community. She passed on this passion for horses to her daughter, who has in return rekindled Isabel's efforts to raise horses. The two mares in her pasture were rescued from the slaughterhouse on her daughter's urging and bred into a herd of Appaloosas on the Nez Perce Reservation.

Quite a few rodeo queens from the 1950s had bonds with horses that shaped the way they looked at themselves, their families, and their communities. Their year as rodeo queen was hardly worth talking about at all. It had fallen away like so many other memories of youth. It was the horses that stayed, not the rodeo. The horses were the bass notes in their lives. The horses were the way to understand what they believed in and how they wanted to live. The horses brought balance, centering their day in the simple act of riding. Time with their horses was time to step away from the pressures of work and family, time to breathe, listen, and wake up to their body.

One rodeo queen sighed when she talked about how she had gone through adolescence on her horse. As a young woman, she would head out to spend hours in the nearby hills and ravines, sometimes leaving right after school and not returning until dusk. "When I was growing up, it was my primary escape. Instead of doing drugs or drinking and stuff like that I can remember sobbing a great many times over lost love on the neck of my horse. I can also remember long and very introspective explorations with my good friends when we would ride. And sometimes we would ride after school until dark all through the hills of Clarkston, up through the Orchards, up on the Heights. And we would just ride, ride on our horses, and it wasn't that we were doing horses as much it was an uninterrupted opportunity to communicate with each other."

I have often wondered what these women would have done without their horses. Many were not ranch women, but children of rural towns and small farms. Growing up with horses at friends and relatives' houses, or at a nearby barn, many queens in the 1950s had the leisure and inclination to make the horse the center of their social and recreational lives. The horse became a means for them to learn about themselves and what they were capable of outside the fairly predictable world of growing up a woman in the 1950s. It gave them freedom.

Few of these women, however, had kept their connection to horses past their young twenties. Isabel was a rare case. She saw ways to make horses not only part of her own life and her daughter's but also part of her community and its relationship with the nearby Nez Perce Reservation. With the help of many volunteers, she is working with the Young Horseman's Program at Lapwai, Idaho, to continue the long process of restoring horse culture to the Nez Perce people. "I have promoted the idea that horses have a very meaningful value for young people as they are growing up and helping them develop an understanding of relationships, responsibility, time management, engaging in good wholesome kinds of activities and feeding back to them appreciation, love, maybe some things that are very important, maybe more important to women—to be loved by an animal."

Working in the Upward Bound program since the 1970s, Isabel has seen cycles of unemployment and despair seize the Nez Perce community. She wants to create opportunities for young Nez Perce, to open the way for them to feel the strength of their traditions and help them navigate the complex world of contemporary America. Horses are the link. They are a means of instilling knowledge and communal identity. She believes that with the right support from community and family, young people can learn through their contact and training with horses basic ways to understand themselves and the world within which they live. Young people who had never ridden a horse before are now rightfully proud of their skill as trail guides and trainers.

During one week, all Isabel's students rode the trail that Chief Joseph took when he fled with his band into Montana away from the pursuing cavalry. Organized by Rudy Shebala, who managed the Nez Perce horse-breeding program, the trail ride did more than provide a momentary escape from the classroom. "The first ride we went on was rainy," Isabel recalled. "There was a mistiness about it, and we were up on the Musselshell . . . I was riding almost at the end of the line of horses. Way up on the trail I could hear the song from Rudy floating back through the mist and the trees. He was chanting a native song that he knew. It was very inspiring, and to know that Chief Joseph crossed this way himself a hundred and some years ago. Not very long. An arm's length back. You could almost reach back and touch the generations involved there. Our history is so close to us. We stand and reach to it."

Many Nez Perce tribal members support this community effort to reclaim horse culture. In a *New York Times* article, Angel McFarland said that to the Nez Perce, "the loss of horses was the loss of a good friend, like losing a dog. It's similar to taking away our braids, our strength, and with the horses, we have that strength back." Horace Axtell, a tribal elder, remembered that his great-grandfather was called Man of the Horses. "He would walk a circle around his horses and they wouldn't leave it." For the Nez Perce, raising horses was a means to reconnect with this ancestral past.

In addition to developing horse herds on the reservation and providing a connection to the Nez Perce past, the Young Horseman's Program offered focus and excitement for young Nez Perce. "I would like to think in ten years it would really be making an impact on the reservation," Isabel said. She felt that young people on and off the reservation had a yearning for experience and a head full of MTV. How did they align TV images with the realities of their daily life? For Isabel, the horse became a means to dispel the self-absorption of TV and present tangible challenges and joys. The horse literally changed the world.

Isabel's work with the Nez Perce is an anomaly among the white rodeo queens I met. Many did not want to talk about the Indians and dismissed the subject. A few admitted they grew up in a racist world, and one woman even told me her parents had one taboo in their house: No dating or socializing with Indians. Some felt guilty. One queen from the 1950s told me she remembered "the old ones [Indians] on the streets of Lewiston going along with their blankets and beads. The men all wear those big ten-gallon hats and moccasins. I always thought they were such sad displaced people. They were then. Some of the old ones, they were with Chief Joseph when they were little babies or little children or their mothers and dads were with Chief Joseph. They were displaced, sad displaced people. It's time they took their place in the world."

There is irony, of course, in her words, because the Nez Perce were in their homeland when they walked the streets of Lewiston. They were not displaced. But they had lost control of their homeland through a sequence of treaties and federal acts. Local business interests and the political actions of miners and ranchers had further helped to carve up their ancestral lands into bits and pieces. The Nez Perce elders in Lewiston no longer held legal, political, or economic power.

Isabel believed that what she learned through her years of working with horses had made her a better citizen, responsive and responsible to her community. It was not about the fleeting celebrity glow of rodeo glory. Or the victory of winning or losing in eight seconds. It was about commitment to place and community, to social justice and tangible rewards. It was about learning respect for the people and animals with which she lived.

The barn was damp cold. The filtered light from the cracks in the arena walls offered no warmth. Horses' heads were hidden in the shadows of their stalls, waiting for morning hay. Madge did not want her horse cooped up in a stall, not even in the winter months, and preferred to have her mare laze away the day under the cluster of locusts or find protection at night in a three-sided corral. The walk leading out to the pasture was crusted thick with lumps of frozen mud. Even the halter, when she picked it up near the gate, was wet to the touch and stiff. She had to push herself to lift up the heavy metal gate and stood muttering as she clumsily reattached the hook. Gates always had a way of shifting, as if the earth were constantly moving under them. Just this once, she wished the latch would shut easily.

She saw the herd in the distance as she swung around and jumped over a narrow stream of iced-over water. She was freezing and in a hurry to halter the bay mare and begin her morning ride. It wasn't going to be easy. No horse ran up to her this morning shaking her head with a hurried whinny. The herd stood scattered over a few dozen yards waiting for her to trudge across the pasture to them. Some days were better than others. Some mornings the bay would lift her head with a bolt and trot right up to her. She didn't know if it was the carrot in her pocket or the rides they had over the harvested fields that would draw her to come.

The sun was higher now and sending light off the patches of ice crisscrossing the pasture. The light off the bay mare almost shimmered as she stood away from her black and chestnut neighbors. Head down to protect against the wind, Madge set off toward the mare. She had walked about fifty yards when she felt the herd start toward her, slowly at first, and then more alert, bumping and pushing each other as they came. She saw the roan twirl and kick up its heels at the small black-and-white Appaloosa, missing by inches the old gelding's haunches. Two of the horses on the edge picked up the pace and galloped off away from her on a diagonal. Within seconds, they stopped and rejoined the herd moving slowly toward the center of the pasture.

She met them with her halter, wondering what they thought of her presence on this frosty morning. They looked expectant, waiting, she thought, for grain or treats. She had none, having forgotten the bag of carrots in the refrigerator she had bought yesterday on sale at the supermarket. The bay mare came up beside her, and Madge quickly flipped the lead line over her head while slipping the halter over her muzzle. Slowly, she led the mare back to the barn, past the irritating gate, over the rocky mud. Back to bridle, bit, and saddle.

The routine had been repeated for years. The riding a balanced dance, floating above the chips and straw of the arena floor or the cracked paths snaking over the hills. The rush over the land, the free gallop, her body leaning over the withers, resting in the wind. No friction, no pushing, no pulling. Some days were like a fight she knew she would never win, her body tense and unresponsive.

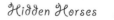

The mare was always quicker than her body, responding to her stiffness and the burdens of her day. Madge's mind interfered with her riding. Her day interfered with her riding. Her life interfered with her riding. Sometimes she wondered about the patience of the horse and the way the mare forgave her inability to be there, simply riding. Maybe that was why she kept coming back: to understand how to make it right, to be there without fear, expectation, or blame. This daily practice anchored her in place.

Madge is a template of several rodeo queens I interviewed. They wanted me to understand what the riding was like. I observed them in the barn, working long hours without the buckle prizes or fast pace of the rodeo world. They wanted me to understand that riding was not a spectator sport. It was a relationship shaped by listening and listening again.

The thrill of the rodeo faded in comparison to the touch and rhythm of everyday life lived with horses. The glow of the rodeo queen paled in comparison to working with their hands, graining the brood mare, and hauling fresh green timothy grass. What Isabel and Madge celebrated was the lifelong choice to live hinged to the needs of animals—to understand that commitment and to see in it a means to restore the self, renew community, and discover a daily practice. The horse connected them to the land, deepening their awareness of who they were, where they lived, and why they were alive.

Separate Belongings

Cracked hooves hit the pavement hard, sending asphalt echoes down the main street of this small eastern Oregon town. Perched on pickups, lawn chairs, and store stoops, the crowd lurched forward as the small herd of horses ran in a lazy lope past their straining heads. The horses promised a taste of the wild but instead reflected hesitancy and caution. Bunched together and nervous, they moved timidly forward. A group of locals ran herd on them, hoping no strays would wander off and frighten the kids and moms spread out along the sidewalk.

The rodeo queen and princess pressed in among the cowboys working the herd. Dressed in starched jeans and beige denim shirts, they helped drive the horses between the gauntlet of people waving and shooting photos. Photographers on the roof of a bank worked fast, hoping to capture the energy of the horses galloping through town. The horses only half obliged, looking reluctant rather than wild.

High overhead an eagle floated, its upturned wings steadfast against the wind. Surprised by its unexpected appearance, the rodeo announcer asked the crowd to look up and gaze at what he called a sign, a clear blessing on the rodeo. Everyone looked up, scanning the sky for a glimpse of the dark form with its white blazing head. It was easy to spot against the clear blue. Even at that height it looked enormous. It circled for minutes, slowly floating over the downtown as if curious about the day's events. Then it headed off, leaving the crowd to return its gaze to the now empty street and wait for the rodeo parade.

Within minutes, a lone Nez Perce Indian rode his horse slowly down the center of town, followed by homemade floats and startled teenage band players, edgy about their musical skills. The annual end of July rodeo had officially begun. Started in 1945, Chief Joseph Days had as its logo Chief Joseph, a Nez Perce from the Wallowa Band, who was hunted down by General Howard in 1877, was exiled with his resistant cluster of Indians to reservations in Oklahoma and northern Washington, and was never again allowed to live in Wallowa County. For his entire life, he refused to accept an allotment on the reservation to the north at Lapwai, Idaho, and he never let go of his right to claim his band's ancestral homeland in the Wallowas. His presence in most of the rodeo promotion was strictly decorative, his face splashed across T-shirts, banners, and flyers stuck up all over the town, his life and struggles submerged beneath the gaiety of community building.

I had come to Joseph to watch the parade and attend a fiftieth reunion lunch for rodeo royalty. I had been warned by rodeo fans that every July, the town suffered from rodeo fever. Dedicated locals put in reams of time to pull off the rodeo and the community breakfasts, lunches, and evening musical events surrounding it. Huge numbers of people drove over from Portland to party hard and dance to cowboy music in the few bars downtown. People in the community had also cautioned me to tread carefully. There were complex politics beneath the surface gaiety. The history of Nez Perce involvement in the rodeo was fraught with a cold-war tension. There had been moments of strain, cooperation, compromise, and rejection. Trust between the rodeo organization and the tribe had wavered over the years without lasting reconciliation.

When I arrived at the luncheon, I was hit by a big dose of small-town pride. Volunteers had worked hard to decorate the community center, turning a plain open hall into a rocking display of balloons, glitter, and Western Americana. In the entranceway, scrapbooks and photographs were spread out on long tables. Fifty years' worth of rodeo queens and princesses greeted each other with stories about children and grandchildren. Many were shocked by the changes the years had made; others had the easy reassurance of seeing friends they ran into every day.

I sat down at a table and joined in the conversation about the current rodeo court and how everyone loved their outfits of beige buckskin. The noise at the tables quieted when the host asked individuals to go to the front of the hall and talk about their experiences as a rodeo queen or princess. Some were embarrassed and said only a few words. Others reminisced about the crazy times, the silly traumas over hairstyles, and the royalty outfits of white gabardine or chartreuse polyester they could no longer even think about wearing. Almost everybody laughed and said how much they loved promoting the rodeo and how they were having a ball reminiscing with old friends.

In the midst of the merriment, a rodeo queen from 1952 said something that broke the mood of lightness. She wished that Patti, the honorary Indian princess connected to her court, was at the luncheon. She had hoped they could meet again. She had never forgotten the beauty of Patti's voice and had always felt this Indian woman deserved to be queen, not her. There was a moment of nervous silence, and then the rustle of clothing and slide of luncheon plates resumed.

After the reunion, I asked around if anyone knew how to get in touch with Patti. Most people I talked with claimed that they didn't know how to contact her, though I found out later that her family were Nez Perce living in nearby Lapwai, Idaho, where Patti's father had been mayor for twenty years. She worked for a local newspaper and was definitely not invisible.

After several phone calls, I tracked Patti down and we arranged to meet at my house. Over the next few months, we had several meetings, sitting in my kitchen over coffee and diet soda. Thoughtful and articulate, Patti knew rodeo better than most queens I had interviewed. A small, deliberate woman, she spoke about her life with clarity and gentleness. Unhurried, Patti would look out over my backyard and smile at my dogs roughhousing in the dirt. She would fold her hands together softly on the kitchen table and smile at my questions. Her calmness made me take the time to talk more carefully. She also surprised me. When she first came over, she drove up in a vintage red Thunderbird.

In 1952, Patti was asked by Walter Brennan, the Western movie star, to help promote Chief Joseph Days as honorary Indian princess. She agreed for specific reasons. She respected Walter Brennan for his knowledge and respect of the Nez Perce. She still remembered one evening at Chief Joseph Days years before when he spoke from the heart about the Nez Perce and recited in the middle of the rodeo arena a narrative about their history. He understood that the Nez Perce belonged to Wallowa County even though they had been exiled for over 100 years. Patti could not remember exactly how she first met Walter Brennan, but she did remember that his attitude toward her and her people made them quickly become friends. After that, whenever he asked her to help him promote the rodeo, she did.

Patti grew up riding her horse and roaming the hills on Webb Ridge, south of Lapwai, the tribal headquarters of the Nez Perce nation, not far from places called Soldiers Meadow, Captain Lewis Rapids, and Mission Creek. Webb Ridge looked down into a sparse creek bed, where locusts clustered around a handful of homes and willows clung tenaciously to a small trickle of water. In late August in these draws, even the berries could seem burned out. Cottonwoods tumbled down cracks in the deeply crevassed hills, shaded dark green and cranberry with withered leaves. But growing up, Patti barely noticed the dry August heat. She and her siblings had lived in Webb and Lapwai Creeks all summer, every summer.

Unlike the land a few miles north where wheat fields carve up the rhythmic hills, turning the earth hard and covered with furrows of eroding soil, the dirt here was more acidic and kinder to sage, scrub brush, and ponderosas. Higher up the ridge, blackberry bushes and chokecherries signaled more water, and the angle of light was less harsh and more forgiving to poplars and elderberries. Whenever I have hiked these draws in late summer, everything looked parched, as if the water had been sucked out of roots and bark. To Patti, the opposite was true. This soil was to her a living abundance. "Drop a seed and it grows," she said. I remembered seeing photos of turn-of-the-century gardens cultivated by Nez Perce women along the Clearwater River. Plowed under by rapacious railroad companies, the gardens had vanished overnight.

Patti grew up in steep canyons where Nez Perce stories shaped the landscape. Many outcroppings and rocky shapes that swelled up into sets of hills and ravines turned into mythic and mischievous characters in Patti's traditional legends. Ant and Yellowjacket wrestled each other in the stone of these hills. Pieces of Monster's Heart were scattered and buried in the rock. The soil sang with stories.

By the time Patti met Walter Brennan and heard him talk about the Nez Perce, she had traveled far from her homeland. At seventeen, she was already an expert at promoting rodeo. The year before, she had been chosen Queen of the West and had spent several months in New York City on radio and television shows, in schools, and at press clubs talking about the National Finals Rodeo in Madison Square Garden. She returned to New York for two more years during the rodeo season as a sponsor girl. There wasn't much she didn't know about rodeo. "To me, from where I stood, it just was like show business. That might have been because some of the people that I enjoyed and got to know better than others were trick riders and clowns, and they were definitely show."

Since she was a young child, Patti and her family had made annual pilgrimages to two regional rodeos with ties to the local Indian communities, the roundups at Pendleton and Lewiston. In the 1930s and 1940s, Indians used Pendleton and Lewiston as occasions to gather together for feasting, bone games, catching up with family, making new friends, and maybe earning extra money by working for the rodeo, riding in the parade and Grand Entry and performing ceremonial dances between the rodeo events. Her father joked about how involved the Indians were in the early years. "Well, you know what my father used to say: If you were ever going to rob any house on the reservation, all you would have to do is get a calendar and say, 'The Lewiston rodeo is here,' because everybody would go. And even people who didn't have cars would catch a ride with somebody and go."

Patti remembered those Indian gatherings next to the rodeo as times of caring. The people always made sure that no one was left alone without food and space to sleep. "People who didn't have teepees would go along because teepees hold a lot of people and so there was always a place you could find to sleep. . . . When we went to Pendleton, we would always find people in our teepee that we didn't know. Wake up in the morning, and there would just be people. Somebody would be walking around at night and say, 'Well, I am looking for this person and I've been all around here.' And my mother would say, 'Well, it's really too dark to be out walking around so why don't you just bring your bedroll in and lay down.'"

Patti brought these experiences to New York when she went to Madison Square Garden, but she had no illusions about the differences between small-town and big-city rodeo. From the start, she knew that her Indian image would be exploited for the business of rodeo. "You are a commodity," she said bluntly. Although her memories of working for the rodeo on a national level still hinged on a positive sense of belonging to a family of rodeo performers, she was absolutely certain that the rodeo, like the rest of America, was about big business. There had been and still was no connection between the rodeo and what the West was actually about; rodeo was fantasy, fun, and excitement.

But for Patti, there was also the joy of artistic exchange. She had exceptional musical talent that people on the reservation and in Lewiston had noticed fast. She had started taking voice lessons at twelve and was encouraged to gain experience outside the rural Northwest. Before she left for New York, she had already traveled to Seattle and Portland with her parents, but nothing had prepared her for the train trip across country. She rode on the train with a chaperone, four women from Pendleton, and Miss Hawaii. Many of the young women she met on the journey dreamed of glamorous lives as models in the big city. She was the only Indian woman in the group.

Her first reaction to New York was total shock. But she never panicked. Looking back on her sixteen-year-old self, she was amazed that she slipped so easily into the frenzy of press briefings, hurried lunches, and spots on radio and television. Her calmness had carried her through. Besides, she understood that she had a chance to test her talent in the entertainment business and the emerging world of television. Patti gained exposure and experience in singing; the rodeo gained a powerful spokesperson.

"I felt strongly I was chosen because I had a talent, and they were into publicizing the rodeo. A lot of places they would go—television shows, schools, and you know, to the press club get-togethers—were places that you couldn't take a horse." For Patti, those three rodeo seasons in New York were opportunities to develop her voice and explore the capital of show business.

What was remarkable to me about Patti's adventure was how she always insisted that her family helped her to understand the experiences she was going through. Rather than prescribe a set of rules, her family tried to think together about choices facing Patti. All her decisions to work with the rodeo had been carefully thought through with her parents. Her parents and grandparents instilled in her a powerful sense of self and tribe, and her rodeo life was never separate from the web of her family relations. She could see clearly how the business of rodeo worked to create commodities, but the rodeo promoters' actions did not tear away at how she lived her life. She knew who she was. She never felt isolated or alone.

Before she left for New York, Patti's father had sat down with her and explained, "If anything bothers you, you can come home. You don't have to put up with anything you don't want." He was clear and utterly convincing. She had to understand that going to New York was business. If the business of rodeo offended her or compromised her sense of herself, she should not participate in it.

Patti conveyed a sense of lightness about her years working for the rodeo. She was acutely aware that she was representing the community of Lapwai, her Nez Perce Indian community, but the responsibility of this representation was not burdensome. She was at ease because her community supported her without question, "down to the last little old lady." Perhaps this connection to her Nez Perce community made it easier for her to keep her perspective in New York and understand that she and the other sponsor girls would have limited roles at the National Finals Rodeo. "I never ever thought for a moment that we were anything but window dressing. And so that's what we did. We showed up. We rode across the arena when our names were announced. We sat in a box and waved at people." She knew that her role in New York was decorative and contained, the dressing around the window, not the world seen through the window.

When I asked her if the newspaper coverage of her in New York was fair and accurate, she replied that on the whole it was, but there was an occasional desire to sensationalize her image, to give the impression she was isolated from American society. "They would lean very, very heavy on the fact that I grew up on a reservation and suggested that I might be really afraid of people with white skin. And suggest that the clothes that I was wearing to press parties, which was often buckskin and beads, was what I wore every day. That was kind of funny. Playing to the Hollywood movies."

At sixteen, before her parents even had a TV, Patti appeared on the *Arthur Godfrey Show,* singing in an amateur talent contest. She remembered the intense heat of the hot lights in the TV studios but had trouble remembering exactly what song she sang. She was never intimidated by TV, but she admitted that the pace was so fast and hard that her desire to make it in the big city dissipated over her three years in New York. She even auditioned for the role of the young Indian woman, Princess SummerFallWinterSpring, on the immensely popular new children's hour, *The Howdy Doody Show,* but was turned down because she was "too sultry."

When she visited schools in New York and Boston, she periodically ran into another Hollywood version of the Indian. "The children in the East were absolutely awed by seeing a woman dressed in buckskin and beads because they just honestly thought that when Indians were dressed like that they were dangerous . . . I just told them about how my life had been, and how I lived in the country and that this is a typical day and that is what I did." This ethnographic encasement in which Indian cultures and their representatives were treated as exhibits from a cultural past was probably the most sophisticated form of silencing Indian peoples. It still is. Removed from the modern, they become perpetual symbols of the original American West. They are expected to act the part of primitives, building longhouses and tanning hides. Or they are depicted as the degraded victims of modernity, drunk and lost on New Mexico highways. Either way, their voices are leveled into the thin cant of nostalgia or fear.

Patti was very well aware that the white community's desire to have Indians participate in rodeos or other cultural events was largely motivated by profit and commercialism. People who came to rodeos expected to see cowboys and Indians. Indian encampments were part of the staging of the ritual of the West.

The economic and social benefits to particular Indians could be positive. Like Leah, Patti saw Indian involvement in the early years as a way for people to get beyond racial barricades. "We also recognize an opportunity to allow people to get to know us a little better and maybe appreciate who we are and what we are a little better. And I think that was probably one of the reasons why I was really anxious to be involved in the rodeo . . . I think that I thought it would help."

Patti was not naive about what she was up against in the racial climate of America. She did not expect to improve the image of Indians on a large scale. But she did think she could make a difference. "On a one-to-one, some of the women that I went and lived with in New York, especially the ones from Texas, had never ever associated with anyone who wasn't white with European-type history. . . . Sometimes people are really surprised when you are dressed in that regalia and you speak English. A lot of intelligent, well-educated people said, well, would say things like, 'Isn't it really cold living in those cloth houses and stuff?' Excuse me. And they still could not get over [how] the movies portrayed what Indians were like. They hadn't seen a reservation. They just knew that it was a really poor place. And they thought people pretty much lived in teepees."

Aware of these misperceptions of Indian peoples, Patti thought that her life in New York and her involvement in rodeo would help bridge some of the enormous gaps between people in the United States. Looking back, she saw that individuals changed but society didn't. The white women she worked with as sponsor girls became friends; the rodeo cowboys she knew treated her with respect and admiration; the trick riders welcomed her. What seemed difficult if not impossible was to change group mentalities. On this level, she saw no cause for optimism. The stereotyping continued.

But there were small improvements. To Patti, Indians today have more areas in their lives to explore their Indianness and their place in American society. They are freer to explore their traditional religion and ceremonies. They are freer to explore careers and to foster economic development of their tribes. They are freer to object and take issue. The basic social and economic conditions of Indians are still bleak, but change is happening. Legal-rights advocates, political-action groups, cultural visionaries, and education reformers work every day, both on the reservations and off, to build a livable future for the tribes.

The powwow circuit has transformed the tradition of Indian gatherings at rodeos. The word *powwow* comes from the language of the eastern seaboard's Narraganset tribe and is historically connected with curing ceremonies. Now it refers to an intertribal gathering of competitive dancing and drumming contests. During the nineteenth century, many dances and religious ceremonies of native peoples were banned by the U.S. government. The Ghost Dance, which originated among tribes on the Plains, was one of many dances violently repressed. Thereafter, Indians often danced with white approval and for white amusement. During the twentieth century, with native peoples confined to reservations, intertribal cultural forms emerged. After World War II, tribes gathered at powwows and blended various regional forms of song, drumming, and dance. In the last twenty years, this cultural exchange has accelerated.

At powwows men, women, and children compete for prizes and money. Specific tribes sponsor powwows, and Indian peoples come from across the United States and beyond to participate. The dances remain connected to their spiritual and traditional roots but foster intertribal relations. Most powwows are open to the public, but the public is expected to respect and abide by clear rules. Photography is often restricted. There is zero tolerance of alcohol or drugs. For some Indians, the powwow circuit has become the Red Road, a way to restore the spirit.

With the surge of powwow events across the United States and the increasingly corporate control of the rodeo, the links between the two worlds have often broken. Rodeo boards see fewer reasons to negotiate with local tribes. Tribes see little reason to participate in the rodeos. Patti believes that it is the increasingly commercial nature of the rodeo that has broken ties between the whites and Indians. "I think that some communities, some rodeo-type people, the business people, said, 'What do we need to pay those people for? Why do we even need them?' And so then they made it hard for Indian people to find a place to camp. They would say, 'We don't want Indian people camping here,' and so they had to find another place. I think that has changed and is changing now. So I have to believe that the people now who are in charge are maybe appreciating a little bit more what Indian people can bring to their show." Some Indians also criticize the powwow circuit as increasingly commercial and shaped by forms of spectatorship. But for Patti, the powwow is still a setting for family reunions where valuable lessons about life are passed on. The values of sharing and exchange, the gossip and romancing, the storytelling and feasting remain part of the powwow circuit. Food and gifts are still given away; child rearing is shared.

Patti saw the earlier Indian encampments at rodeos as precursors of the present-day powwow circuit. "I remember how everybody shared everything. You could go there without a dime and you would eat well and be treated really well." Her son reminded her that this tradition still continues today. He told her a story about how his wife was at first alarmed with all the offers to help with her children when she showed up at the powwows. She had to open up her concept of the family. And whenever he shows up alone with the children, he is swarmed by elders offering to help. Patti looked at me, "I think it is a teaching of the next generation of how things should be." Later she added, "It is like a family reunion. You always know that whenever you go to a certain place these are people you are going to see. And before we leave one place we'll be packing up and all of the people who have camped around us would say, 'Are you going to Wellpinit this year? Well, we will see you there.' The children always exchange things and hope they'll see their friends there . . . It was something I think that Indian people always did. Always had these get-togethers at different places. To live any kind of satisfying life you need get-togethers."

When I was at Joseph for the rodeo and royalty luncheon, I needed a break from the high-pitched hysteria of the rodeo events. I walked away from the rodeo grounds toward the irrigation canals that wound through town and found myself at the Indian encampment, a cluster of teepees spread out across a small grassy area. Pickup trucks and RVs were sprinkled throughout the campground. Kids ran around, laughing and shouting; some were cooling off in the water canals. Adults talked over the day's schedule, deciding how to get their regalia over to the high-school auditorium where the dance and drumming contests were in progress.

At midday, the encampment was fairly quiet since almost everyone was over at the high school helping out with the events. The encampment used to be in a vacant lot closer to the rodeo grounds, but that lot had been turned into a retirement community. I knew there were concerns about the future of the encampment and its relation to the rodeo. When I was visiting, everyone I talked with wanted to avoid the issue—too political, too many hard feelings. I felt like an outsider, walking in a minefield. Too much history for one small community.

I made my way over to the auditorium and sat for a few hours watching the dances and listening to the drumming. Some of the dances were outdoors, in a spot where bleachers had been set up around a temporary floor. There were a few tourists standing or sitting, just listening. The dance floor was ringed with plastic folding chairs for the dancers and their families. Groups of drummers shifted their positions around a large drum as they worked their way through the rhythms of a fancy or traditional dance.

Young girls swirled in bright pink and blue shawls. The tingling sound of a jingle dress, covered in small metallic cones, followed a teenager down the steps and onto the dance floor. The Indian princess competition of the powwow was very low-key. The announcer emphasized that all the young women involved were community leaders, attending conferences for the tribe, assisting in educational projects, and showing active participation in their schools. The winner was celebrated with a circle dance to which everyone was invited. The line curved around the dance floor, as people of all ages danced slowly, their feet barely moving above the ground. The odds were that the Indian princess would not be going into town that night for the rodeo dance. Indians and cowboys still did not mix in this town. They inhabited parallel paths and parallel worlds. Their lives did not intersect. For many it was easier that way.

As a young woman, Patti had understood that the Queen of the West was only a transitory role among many she would play in her lifetime. It saddened her that being a rodeo queen was or could be the most significant moment in a woman's life. Her community valued her as an individual before and after she became Queen of the West. She always had a sense that she was special. Her family and community gave her that gift. A rodeo queen might be a means but never an end, since what it offered was only a brief, superficial glimpse into an artificial world. To believe in it was an act of foolishness.

When I first met Patti, I asked her if she still went to Chief Joseph Days. She said her family would travel to Joseph but then be tempted away by the allure of Wallowa Lake. The lake held them spellbound. "We get over there, and we get to the lake, and there's something so tempting about being there and sitting around the campfire. And we get up and fix breakfast and fixing breakfast takes a couple of hours, and it seems like we have so much to do during the day, and we have such good times so somehow we just don't get to the rodeo." The land and their closeness held them in place; the town's rodeo fever created hardly a ripple of excitement.

I tried to imagine what it would be like for them, sitting by the water, listening to the occasional hawks overhead hunting for their food, their nests held tight in the tops of dead cottonwoods above marshy edges of the shore. The lake was a nugget of water set at the edges of a moraine drifting from deep green to scaly brown. Walking above it on the trails into the Eagle Cap Wilderness, I always felt its beauty was almost abstract and solitary, its hard edges carved away from tilting land.

Patti talked about how she and her family would sit and watch at the lake's edge, taking pleasure in the cold blue water and light over the mountains they knew had been forbidden to the Wallowa Band of the Nez Perce. The father of Chief Joseph was buried at the foot of the lake. Even his grave was tinged with controversy since the land it rested on was contested for local development. Respect for this elder was mired in rumors of desecration. A dentist in Oregon had boasted for years he had the elder Joseph's skull in his office.

Only recently have the Nez Perce officially returned to the Wallowas. In 1997, they purchased 10,300 acres of land and renamed it Witewisnix Wetes, meaning Precious Land. Patti felt a deep love for this land. And so she enjoyed each minute she cooked breakfast and stayed by the fire, talking with family and friends, feeling the pull of place, its history and beauty. The rodeo could wait.

A year after talking with Patti, I sat in a lush living room looking out over a golf course talking with another woman who, like Patti, loved music, promoted rodeo, and grew up in the Webb Ridge area. We chatted for a few minutes about golf and country

clubs. In her early seventies, Joan still golfed three or four times a
week. Stocky but athletic, she was dressed well in a casual white
summer suit. Her personality was strong. With piercing eyes, she
grilled me about why I was writing a book on rodeo queens. A few
years older than Patti, Joan had been rodeo queen in the late 1940s
and, like many other rodeo queens, remembered what an honor it
was to represent her community. Like Patti, she too had pretty
much stopped her career when she married. Joan shook her head
when she thought about it. She had to "settle down and be a wife."
How the world had changed.

I listened to her talk about her childhood, growing up on a cattle and wheat ranch, fixing three hot meals a day during harvest for
the hired hands, working long days, and riding off with her sisters
in the late afternoon to explore deserted homesteads, Indian cemeteries, and whatever else caught their eyes. Thinking back, she
could not believe the freedom they had been given. People would
never let their kids do those things today. She remembered some
of the deserted houses and the lilacs still blooming in the yards.
Cups and saucers still sat in the kitchen cabinets, and the orchards
out back still held fruit.

In the midst of her stories, she interrupted herself and asked
me, "Have you seen *Horse Whisperer*? That was my life." She was
proud of her memories and how "very brave" everyone had been.
In the next breath, she added that she would never choose to be a
rancher's wife. Her children and husband loved to hear the stories
about her childhood, but, no, she was never meant to stay close to
the ranch, its horses, cattle, dogs, or machinery. She had dreamed
about ballet and travel. She left the land as soon as she could.

I showed her an old photograph I had found in the archives of
the local newspaper. She was leaning against a rock wall, her left
arm swung back to brace her balance, her right hand resting on a
gun belt. She had on a white hat and heavy leather chaps. She

squinted and smiled at the same time, looking out into the distance, a perfect cowgirl gunslinger. It was the only photograph I had in which a rodeo queen wore guns and chaps as if she had walked out of an action-glutted Western movie. Joan was not photographed shooting but was caught in a moment of contemplation. She was armed and waiting. Her manicured fingernails and polished boots contrasted with her heavy gun belt.

I asked Joan how she had felt when the photograph was taken. "It wasn't me. It was the first time I ever touted a six-shooter." She told me that the editor of the local newspaper wanted her to look rough and tough like a real cowgirl. "I really wasn't. I was more feminine." She thought the photograph "corny," but she was willing to do what they wanted. Because she came from a ranch, they shaped her into their fantasies of what a "real cowgirl" was like. And she was willing to pose the part. "I didn't care," was all she said.

Whenever I show Joan's photograph in public, people are alarmed at the image of a rodeo queen as gunslinger. Some are amused to see the feminine queen transformed into the masculine fighter. Others are dismayed to see a woman gone butch. Joan thought the pose was the photographer's fantasy. She tried to distance herself from the photograph, claiming her femininity in the face of the photographer's drive to cross-dress her for the camera. She was uncomfortable about the gender confusion and talked repeatedly during the conversation about homosexuals and how they were taking over the world. She clearly wanted the lines separating men and women to be clear. The gender roles prescribed in the 1950s had demanded this clarity. She seemed to still agree.

After lunch we talked about how the ranch world of her childhood overlapped with the rodeo. Her father had died when she was a young teenager, cutting her out of the power structure of the town. In the 1950s, a young woman became a rodeo queen by having her father on the rodeo board. In Joan's case, the "Western elite" of her small town discovered her when she moved into town and started working and playing piano for a local band. After she became queen, she would walk down the street and feel how people noticed her. It was exciting.

When I asked her about local Indian involvement in her rodeo, Joan's tone changed. She paused, recalling how she felt when she was young. Joan had grown up on the Nez Perce Reservation close to where Patti had lived and used to ride. Joan went to the nearby school on Mission Creek and remembered with awe the Nez Perce Indian Paul Slickpoo, with his tall black hat and blanketed shoulders, who, she said, had been in Chief Joseph's army. "My concept of Nez Perce Indians was never very complimentary," she said. "We leased a lot of our land from Indians. It was so normal to see an Indian car in the driveway." Then come stories of money lending and politics. "They never could wait till their payments came in and my father always gave them something—part of his goodwill—because they could change at a whim and lease it to somebody else."

The Indian world and Joan's social world never overlapped, though she lived on or near Indian land throughout her childhood. She and her friends used to "sneak around" the sweat baths and Indian cemeteries. She had to admit, though, that "we were all spooked and scared to death of those Indians." When she was young, she thought that Indians were not ambitious and not "progressive," a curious choice of words since the Nez Perce have been described as divided between progressives and traditionalists by outsider anthropologists and missionaries for decades. Joan was quick to add in the midst of her litany of criticisms that "we always ruined the Indian because I think they were good people before we took over and put them on a reservation." Once on the reservation, they seemed to have had no will to resist deterioration. In a real sense, Joan saw them as being without any self-determination or ability to act.

Webb Ridge and Mission Creek were an intimate world of creek beds, canyons, and niches of rich soil where gardens grew. It was inconceivable to me that anyone could grow up here and not know everything about the neighbors. Maybe my Chicago upbringing has made me immune to the ways in which the rural West could erect such cunning walls to divide its people.

When I asked about Nez Perce involvement in her rodeo, Joan could not remember a single thing, not even if there had been Indians in the parade. In response to my question about whether Indians and whites could use the rodeo as a meeting ground, she replied forcefully: "I don't see rodeo as a place to get to know anybody." Yet meeting people was a big part of why Joan enjoyed her year as rodeo queen. In the 1950s, rodeo queens partied at the country clubs and chamber functions. Her world and the Nez Perce world were as separate as the Soviet Union and United States of the 1950s. Everyone watched, everyone maneuvered, but nobody tried to know the other.

I asked Joan if she had moved in the social world of the rodeo cowboys or if, like other rodeo queens, she had been shielded from their wild ways. Joan said she had hung out with the boys but had not liked most of their rough ways. But there was one exception, Casey Tibbs, the famous saddle-bronc champion, featured on the cover of *Life* magazine in 1951. Casey would come a-wooing. He alone of the group was a rodeo cowboy and a gentleman. "But then you must know Patti," I said. (Patti knew Casey Tibbs, I kept thinking. There must be a connection between Patti and Joan.) "Patti?" She responded. Never heard the name.

Two women lived in the same place, loved music, rode horses, and found charm in rodeo and Casey Tibbs. Two women became symbols of the American West, rode in parades, and saluted the flag. Two women found that marriage meant settling down and a letting go of dreams. Two women lived in separate worlds.

Queen Betty, 1931

Joan, Lewiston Roundup, 1949

JoAnne, 1945

Lewiston Roundup, 1947

Leah with President Harry S. Truman, Pendleton Round Up, 1952

Jean, Lewiston
Roundup, 1954

Jean, publicity shot for
Lewiston Roundup, 1954

Chief Joseph Days
Court, 1953

Susan receiving prize
from Bob Barker,
Miss Rodeo America, 1959

Miss Rodeo America
competition,
Flamingo Hotel,
Las Vegas, 1959

Lewiston Roundup, 1976

Lewiston Roundup Promotional Shot,
Rodeo Court with Slim Pickens, 1960s

Lewiston Roundup Queen, 1990

Pendleton Round-Up Parade, 2001

Miss Rodeo America contestants for the 1997 Crown

Rhinestone Cowgirls

"W as it about Vietnam?"

I was sitting in a long narrow room off a banquet hall in the Flamingo Hotel. A former Miss Rodeo America asked me this question. At first, I did not hear her. I had come to Las Vegas to talk with the new contestants for the Miss Rodeo America title but had also ended up meeting with several former Miss Rodeo Americas. The woman sitting across from me has been active in the national pageant for forty years. I had just asked her why in the 1960s and 1970s, the understated look of Western gabardine suits had transformed into the rhinestone glitter of Las Vegas. Had rodeo queens become showgirls? By the end of the 1970s, it was all big hats, big hair, rhinestone tiaras, and Liberace sequins.

The question was beginning to get me down; I had asked it so often. "Why all the glitter?"

She shot back again, "Was it about Vietnam?"

One hairdresser I knew who worked with rodeo people thought the change had come about through some bizarre mix of the Jackie Kennedy bouffant style and the pompadours of Elvis Presley.

Working-class America was reaching out for signs of wealth and had ended up mixing the tasteless with the trappings of power. Hair spray for the masses.

I also knew that in the 1960s, Nudie Cohen, the rodeo tailor from Hollywood, had dressed Country Western singing stars in rhinestones, and the style had caught on. Diamonds for the masses. What's more, the Miss Rodeo America pageant moved to Las Vegas in 1958 from conservative Oklahoma City, mixing dance-girl glitter with cowboy glitz. Sequins for everybody.

But Vietnam? I was taken aback by her question. What did Vietnam have to do with it? Had all the disorderly long hair of the hippies, Weathermen, and liberation armies prompted the rodeo world to reply with the innocence of extreme Shirley Temple curls? Had the androgynous 1960s sparked a need for gender exaggeration, and had the rodeo out-trumped men with long hair by requiring women to reclaim their femininity with mounds of fluff?

Hair became everything in the late 1960s. It defined you. Once when I was camping in Glacier Park in the northeastern corner of Montana, a young man walked over to my tent site at dawn. I was making morning coffee. Everything in the camp was nearly frozen, my washcloth stiff as cardboard. I looked at him for a few moments and noticed that his hair was long on one side and short on the other. He looked tired and edgy. He started to talk about how he had been jumped in a bar in a small town near the park and beaten up by some cowboys who threw him down behind the bar and started to cut his hair. I don't remember how he got away.

Montana that summer was not the fun, carefree place of my youth. I was driving a beat-up Volkswagen with eleven dents and Massachusetts plates, and I was worried. At the Montana-Canadian border, every inch of my car was searched and the bags of herbal tea tucked in the glove compartment confiscated for lab analysis. The world was changing.

In the 1960s, many of my peers and I began to see cowboys as reactionaries. They stood for a new, vehement patriotism, and if you didn't agree with their politics, you better get out of their way. Of course, many of my cowboy friends would say those were just wanna-be cowboys, vigilantes hanging out in the local bar acting tough or coming down hard at a small Montana border crossing. Having fun, harassing hippies.

I remembered the cowboys I had known as a child in Colorado, gentlemen who dressed up in their string ties and walked downtown with their wives on their arms. But maybe they were only well behaved in front of the ladies and those who looked, acted, and behaved like them. Maybe they couldn't and wouldn't tolerate difference, and the gun was only too handy to right what seemed like social wrong.

In my view, by 1966, President Lyndon Johnson's cowboy diplomacy stood for an abusive foreign policy, dragging many people into a war that would divide Americans, splitting up families and making public the social rifts in American society. Young girls raised in the 1950s put away their bobby socks, bangs, and crinoline skirts and started protesting the Vietnam War and asserting their rights as women. They grew their hair long and straight, defying those cute flipped-up pageboys that Doris Day made immortal. Male heroes were chunked, too. Gene Autry and his cowboy code could no longer attract their attention. Cowboys had become duplicitous antiheroes, even villains.

When I interviewed rodeo queens who were closer to my age and had lived through the 1960s, I had a difficult time understanding how and why they had resisted these social changes. Many rodeo queens had no desire to tamper with the cowboy code. In fact, they fought to preserve it. Many wanted a more adamant American rodeo that kept core values like hard work, strong morals, patriotism, and traditional gender roles alive.

But there was trouble brewing. The affluence of the 1960s and 1970s had increased the class divisions in their small towns and had hurt them. And they were angry that it cost too much money to become the town's rodeo queen. To some, big money was ruining rodeo altogether. Rodeo clamored for advertising and corporate sponsors like a two-bit whore. But rodeo at its best was still the heart of America, despite the dwindling audiences in the 1960s. Nothing could change their loyalty to rodeo. Not even the loss of the rural West. All the queens I talked with in the 1960s and 1970s lived in town. Most knew about ranching and farming from their parents or grandparents. The others came from families that had sold out before they became queens. Their old West had disappeared, vanishing underneath cities, suburbs, and tacky trailer courts.

In the 1960s, I too believed that big money was destroying America. Fattened by military contracts, corporations like Dow Chemical and DuPont produced Agent Orange, cluster bombs, and napalm to use against Southeast Asian civilians. Big money also played its part in the loss of rural lands, turning farmland into ski resorts, agribusiness, and urban sprawl. But I made a different equation than the rodeo queens and kicked the cowboy out. Macho masculinity laced with moral righteousness and corporate greed was too deadly a blend. Bring on the long hair for men, I shouted. Maybe that might confuse gender roles just enough to lessen the violence. Of course, it was not that easy.

Most of the women I talked with who were queens in the 1960s and 1970s did not want to talk about national politics at all. The issues that pained them about rodeo were local. Extreme competition, the hunt for status, the pressure for dollars, or the loss of community support tainted but did not destroy the rodeo. Most had never faltered in their belief in the rodeo as an honorable road to core American values. Conservative roles for men and women were necessary to keep the world steady.

If they did sever the rodeo from the heart of America, they did so by claiming that rodeo was a professional sport, freed of American symbols and class tensions altogether. Rodeo was an athletic contest, period. As a sports event, it had no connection to the ranching West at all. Rodeo queens had serious jobs as business promoters. Their work was upgraded in the corporate-sponsored rodeo arena. Even the word *queen* rankled. She was better described as a corporate icon, a team leader, a businesswoman, or even a diplomat for the sport of rodeo.

Rodeo queens also had opportunities for more work. By the mid-1970s, the professional world of rodeo had changed to accommodate women athletes. After decades of banishment, women reentered rodeo as competitors, not cheerleaders. After much resistance, women's barrel racing had become a common event in professional rodeo. Some rodeo queens could both promote and compete in the rodeo arena. They had finally arrived.

But why all the big hair? I was giving up on finding a simple answer. The closest I came to one was by remembering the constant refrain of rodeo queens during the 1960s and 1970s: Big money, not big hair, had changed the rodeo world. The show-biz glamour was a symptom of a deeper disturbance. The hair matched the heightened quest for wealth that the 1960s kids had rejected. No dropping out if your hairdo is a mound of gorgeous curls. The conflict was over the money.

Bette, who was a queen in 1962, bemoaned that the local newspaper had lost interest in the rodeo queens by the end of the 1970s. By then, the paper was printing sports statistics about rodeo cowboys and cowgirls rather than feature articles on royalty. The first thing she showed me when I visited her was her scrapbook, packed with newspaper articles, showing her riding, playing the piano, and working around the house. Bette lifted up one dried-out sheet and held it before me. "It was a full-page spread where now it's kind of hard to find the article, to even know who is queen," she protested. Sitting on her cream couch in her modest living room, gently holding her scrapbook, Bette could not take her eyes away from the photos of herself riding her palomino at full tilt and waving her white cowboy hat. "It was quite a dream come true." She touched the edges of the pictures carefully.

Bette talked about how she idolized Miss Rodeo America when she met her at the local rodeo back in 1962. A section of her scrapbook was devoted to this tall, blonde, and blue-eyed beauty with a perfectly shaped pageboy. To Bette, she was the model of the Western woman and the essence of a rodeo queen. She had good manners, was friendly, generous, and always behaved properly. Bette would have loved to become Miss Rodeo Idaho. She was a finalist for the state competition in 1963 but lost out on the glory and the prizes—a special charm bracelet, a leather jacket, a sterling-silver buckle, and a trip to Las Vegas to compete in the Miss Rodeo America contest. For consolation, Bette had her scrapbook, stuffed with cards congratulating her and wishing her well.

An imitation oil portrait of Bette in her full rodeo queen outfit hung on the living room wall. "The community was so good to me. Even that portrait up there was given to me." Her husband, she explained, wanted her portrait out at all times, not hidden away in the bedroom closet. For him, she was still a celebrity. During my interview, he hovered over her as though she was a precious gem.

After all the years, what stayed with Bette was the pride of having the community single her out. "Then, you were chosen. It was an honorable thing. Now it's more a competition." In the 1960s, the rodeo queen was still selected by the rodeo board. Candidates did not have to prove their horse skills or speaking abilities against a crowd of others. In the 1930s they did, but by the 1940s, the rodeo board ruled. By the early 1970s, the method of selecting queens had changed again. There were fewer in-house rodeo committee nominations and more open competitions, involving try-outs and interviews. Despite these changes, the daughters of rodeo promoters, stockmen, and board members often ended up on the rodeo royalty court.

Before I left, I asked Bette how she wanted to be remembered. She said something that took me aback. A soft-spoken, demure woman whose handshake was a slight touch and who had taken time off from her job behind the jewelry counter at a nearby department store to visit with me, Bette wanted to be remembered by the rodeo slogan "She's Wild."

I said good-bye and walked down the concrete steps of her house, shaking my head. There wasn't a wild thing in sight. Tract-style ranch houses and manicured lawns stretched out to my right and left. I tried to imagine Bette charging through the fields on her palomino, but the sharp-edged lawns made wildness disappear.

Kris's memories were similar to Bette's. Animated and fun-loving, Kris had put aside an entire morning to reminisce. Her home was large, shaded by huge elms and maples, in a quiet, upscale section of Spokane. Her small round face was a series of continual big smiles when I was with her, but she told me she had cried over her scrapbook before I came. Looking back and seeing an extinct world was hard. For Kris, becoming rodeo queen in 1966 was a "Cinderella thing." She was like a movie star in town and could "socialize with the elite."

All that glittered was not gold, however. Now you needed big money to become rodeo queen. She might have squeaked by in the

1960s, but no way today. The whole scene had become "distasteful," and the parents were to blame. They pushed too hard, concerned more about outdoing their neighbors than taking care of their kids. Kris had loved horses growing up and had participated in gymkhanas and junior rodeo, but the horse world was getting more competitive and more expensive. If a young woman had the right parents, the right horse, and the right amount of money, she stood a chance at becoming queen. Without these ingredients, she faced tremendous obstacles. Too many people were excluded.

Despite these realities, Kris still thought that rodeo was "Western culture—pure Americana." Through rodeo, she felt a sense of connection to the West of her grandfather, who had been a cowhand and was "part Indian." By 1970, 83 percent of the people in the Mountain and Pacific Coast states lived in urban areas, but for her, rodeo still had its roots in the ranch. The rodeo queens may have moved to the suburbs, but the rodeo was still a way for them to tap into the rural West.

In a long letter she wrote me, Christina, another ex-rodeo queen, remembered that in the middle of the Vietnam War, the American Legion had been seriously promoting the rodeo in her hometown. Rodeo was American, homegrown, and patriotic. When she became rodeo queen in 1970, Christina called herself an ambassador for the sport of rodeo. Her family was not from the small town's business elite. Christina had to work doubly hard to qualify for the tryouts, selling tickets for the rodeo with support from her father. "He took me out after school every single day and on weekends to every single function where people gathered and I sold tickets." Once voted queen on criteria that included the total sale of tickets, her family felt she had to have a new horse. The financial strain was considerable, but worth the sacrifice.

Both Christina and her family gained status with her coronation. In town, "folks regarded me with a kind of admiration and remembered me because I was the Rodeo Queen." Christina remembered one cowboy who became infatuated with her and sent her flowers and a chartreuse cowboy hat. "He seemed very happy when I was with him—like I was some kind of a prize." The public spotlight was intense but useful. Christina gained enough confidence to break the mold of small town life, go on to college, and broaden her horizons. Without the rodeo, she thought she might "have married a hometown boy and reared kids while working at A&W drive-in."

Her gain in self-worth came with social consequences. There were bad feelings from the upper levels of the hierarchy in her small town. "The only thing that seemed to plague me was the underlying current of hostility that resulted when I won the crown instead of a gal who was regarded as being a fine horsewoman and her parents owned a big cattle ranch. She didn't even sell enough tickets to gain the Princess title. So, because I won the competition fair and square, I felt that some people tolerated me . . . and I hung in there proving myself all year long."

Christina felt that her main function was to be a cheerleader for the sport of rodeo. What saved her from thinking about herself as only a cheerleader was that she also rode horses and worked with livestock. She saw rodeo as a "very macho sport—kind of like bullfighting in Spain. . . . It pits skill, agility and physical strength against brute power. I never could understand what drove some cowboys to ride bulls time after time even after they'd be broken, gored or bruised up. I wondered if they really had any common sense. But I figured it was okay to be supportive if they had to do it. Bull riding was always a crowd-pleaser . . . that's why it was the last event of the rodeo . . . to leave the audience with a peak experience."

I never interviewed Christina in person. She had sent me a long letter answering a number of questions I had asked her. When I read these last words, I thought of the 1961 movie *The Misfits*. Set in Reno, Nevada, the movie depicts the West as a backwater for those escaping the lies and deceptions of middle-class society. But the West offers no sanctuary. Instead, cowboys provide erotic fantasies for upper-middle-class women in Reno for the weekend, and rodeo cowboys act like jaded circus-players struggling to be freed from working for wages.

In the movie, Montgomery Clift rodeos because he has lost his right to ranch. His father died and his mother remarried. His new stepfather turned him into a hired hand, and the insult drove him off his home and into the rodeo. Clark Gable, a former working cowboy, plays a cowboy whore for divorcées in Reno, a precursor of the midnight cowboys to come. He lives off the marital and social discord of America and dreams about the old days.

Marilyn Monroe, a recent divorcée, pleads with Montgomery Clift not to go back in the rodeo arena and gamble his body riding bulls. She sees that in his drive to escape his do-nothing job, Clift has fallen into the trap of becoming a gladiator for the masses, willingly sacrificing his body for their entertainment. The crowd just wants blood.

Like Marilyn Monroe, many bull riders' wives and girlfriends I have known have pleaded with their men to stop. The rush is not worth the pain and the damage to their relationship. One ex-bull rider told me that he and his wife had agreed never to go to a rodeo ever again. He did not want to lose her to the temptations of the chute. He was lucky—he had only broken bones to show for his years on the amateur circuit—and he wanted to keep it that way for his wife and his family. Anyway, there was only so much craziness in him.

Unlike Marilyn Monroe, who protested that there shouldn't be a rodeo, Christina believed in the show. She felt the rodeo cowboys represented "the hard-driving American who hangs in there until he succeeds. The American who doesn't give up or ever say 'quit.' Even when it doesn't make any logical sense, they struggle on in the face of adversity, each time honing their skills to make a better ride, a better performance, be the fastest, the best or the most perfect."

A tall lanky woman, Sarah sat in her living room under a large portrait of herself as rodeo queen, painted twenty-five years earlier. Her aging, puffy face contrasted sharply with the huge image of the smiling blond queen above her head. I remembered a 1971 promotional photo of Sarah, having her hair teased by a local beautician. Wrought-iron hooks and horse outlines were scattered throughout the room. On a side wall, a portrait of Jesus Christ stared soberly out over the neo-cattle decor. Sarah insisted that her husband wanted her portrait center stage, but she later mentioned that her parents had a twin oil painting in their living room.

Sarah's mother and father were with her on the rodeo circuit in the early 1970s, helping with her clothes, arranging special events, and finding additional rodeos for her to attend. They had groomed her for the rodeo queen competition for years. She learned how to ride at saddle clubs and pony clubs. She had been in junior rodeos and knew how competition worked. She could not have been queen without her parents' financial and emotional support. "My mother was the one who took me and dressed me. When I went to a horse show, my dad would saddle my horse and my mother would dress me and away we would go." Sarah was always costumed and dressed perfectly as rodeo queen. "My mother, she was very much a lady and to have everything prim and proper would be important to her. . . . She helped us design and figure out what the court wanted to do. . . . The queen always wore white."

Sarah defended the rodeo when I had not even asked for a defense. When I asked her about the cultural context of the 1970s and the changes women's lives were undergoing, she resisted the idea that the rodeo queen was connected to the shift in social roles for women. She felt comfortable with the traditional roles for women. "They worked, didn't they?"

The disruptive sexual behavior of the 1960s was anathema for moral and professional reasons. "Pregnancy. That was a no-no. . . . You were not hanging onto your boyfriends. That was not tolerated. . . . You don't have the time to put into a boyfriend." Queens could not have boyfriends distracting the court from the jobs they had to do for the rodeo. The rodeo court was a professional team completely separate from the rodeo performers. The virgin queens were on a strict work schedule. Western heritage was serious business.

In contrast to Sarah, Mickie, a rodeo queen in 1974, felt the new demands on rodeo queens were destructive. Mickie had stolen a few precious hours to talk with me. A nurse and mother of two small children, she worked hard to keep the household expenses balanced. Throughout our talk, she stressed that the pain came from the increased affluence of a few who made money the main requirement in competition. By the mid-1970s, the number of outfits the rodeo queen needed had skyrocketed. Her parents, the parents of her princesses, and her chaperone had all agreed to resist the new trend. They flatly refused to buy more clothes and travel to more rodeos. They tried to keep the hairstyles simple. Mickie was not sure why the pressure mounted in the 1970s. She did not think it came from the rodeo board, but rather from the parents. Some wanted their daughters to travel to ten to fifteen rodeos a year. The queens rode a "trailer race." Parents with more money poured it into their kids' events. Rodeo queens became display signs for the family. For Mickie, the rodeo became both more commercial and more empty. The rodeo queen waved her arm like a mechanical doll as she rode around the arena.

She remembered riding her horse when she was a young girl over the Snake River hills. Those vetch- and cheat-grass-covered hills were important to her, but much about the rodeo seemed to have become detached from her love of horses or her daily life. She kept saying she did not understand why it happened. Maybe it was the parents; maybe it was corporate America. The local businessmen wanted the sponsorship of corporate giants. Wrangler Jeans, Budweiser, Coors, Dodge Trucks, Skoal/Copenhagen, Justin Boots, Crown Royal Whiskey—they all wanted a piece of the action. The rodeo had lost its moorings in the community, disappearing beneath the ambitions of parents and the corporate strategies of giant companies. Rodeo queens had become fashion statements. Their hair had to flash big, their clothes sparkle. Mickie felt an ordinary family of four couldn't even afford to go to a rodeo; the admission price was too high.

In 1979, the movie *The Electric Horseman*, starring Robert Redford, played in movie theaters across the United States. Redford played Sonny Steele, a World Championship rodeo cowboy. Sonny had become an advertising gimmick. The "Ampco Cowboy," he promoted "Ranch Breakfast" cereal. He would ride into the arena covered with lights like a human billboard. Each rodeo brought further humiliation. Sonny's despair found its expression in booze until he could no longer even ride his horse and was replaced by a stand-in. The audience did not know the difference. Throughout the movie, a popular Willie Nelson song, "Mamas Don't Let Your Babies Grow Up to Be Cowboys," plays in the background.

In the film, Jane Fonda critiques Sonny relentlessly about his exploitation as a corporate icon. Finally, he vindicates himself by escaping on Rising Star, a magnificent horse used by corporate sponsors to promote their products. The horse has been shot with penicillin, tranquilizers, and steroids until he stands, listless, zombie-like, and sterile, a drugged tool of greedy America. Sonny and Rising Star ride off together down the streets of Las Vegas away from the chorus girls and the neon gimmicks. After Sonny releases Rising Star in a lush pasture, he hitchhikes down the road to find "something simple, hard, but plain and quiet." His actions are framed by the lyrics, "I grew up dreamin' of being a cowboy."

***

We don't go to the rodeo with a tube of lipstick anymore," Shauna said. "Most of us have briefcases, itineraries." Almost in the same breath, her mother added that the rodeo board wanted their girls "to walk the straight and narrow." It was getting harder to stay a "good girl" with so many temptations, but the requirement was as forceful as it had been in the 1950s.

The corporate queen had to have a public moral face. No boyfriends hanging on her arm everywhere she went, no drinking in public, no smoking in public, no pregnancy, no marriage, no misbehaving. Middle-class morality was essential no matter how commercial the event was, no matter how much a business the rodeo had become. The queen had to be a role model for the young girls in town. The briefcase in hand was part of the act. It was very hard work.

I talked until late at night with three sisters, Shauna, Sarah, and Jackie, and their mother, Karmen, at a local hangout in Tonasket,

Washington. The sisters had grown up on a ranch in central Washington near the Canadian border, but those ranching days were gone. Strong supporters of their local rodeo, they had participated in regional, state, and national rodeo queen competitions. They were queens in the 1980s and 1990s, but they spoke to the changes happening earlier.

We ate cheeseburgers and argued about the changes in the rodeo and rodeo royalty. The oldest sister, Shauna, an athletic, dark-eyed brunette, defended rodeo all evening long. Her younger sisters, Sarah and Jackie, had more reservations. Their rodeo photos showed them with cascades of blond curls. Only Jackie had kept the hairdo. First they fought over their pioneering past and its connection to rodeo. After some squabbling, the younger sisters won out. Rodeo wasn't ranch reality, but a dream world. It was a Western playground for men and women who were hooked on youth. In sharp contrast, the real world of ranching made you old before your time. Ranching was about loss and poverty, about the drudgery of backbreaking work from early in the morning until late at night. It was about losing and losing again with nobody to bail you out. Ranching was financial tragedy. Not one of them could live off it.

Even though the middle sister, Sarah, did not want the heartbreak of a ranch for her son, she looked to the rodeo to instill in him the values of ranching. She believed passionately in the cowboy way, and she wanted to pass it on. Her two sisters disagreed, saying you can't have it both ways. Rodeo had nothing to do with reality or ranching or the life of the land. There was no such thing as a cowboy without cows. Even the horses had lost their ranch sense. A barrel-racing horse, a team-roping horse, a calf-roping horse, a steer-wrestling horse would be lost in the sagebrush herding cattle. Rodeo horses had been trained in fragmented, specialized ways, and they could no longer work the land. Besides, you would never risk your $50,000 competition barrel horse to pick up a few cows on the rocky ridge. The ranch life was through.

The conversation became hot and angry. Rodeo and its royalty were corrupted by money. You could "buy a win" to become rodeo queen. Horses, training, outfits, and modeling classes all took bucks, all demanded resources to win. All three sisters insisted that the smaller the rodeo, the less of this economic determinism applied. At smaller rodeos, hard work and moral values won out if you were queen, and hard work alone got you the win in the chutes. But the larger the rodeo, the more money mattered. "Whoever has the most money and influence wins," the sisters finally agreed.

If money now ran everything in America, including rodeo and the ranch, what was left to believe in? The younger sisters insisted that rodeoing was no way to live. It was a dream only a handful could realize. Even worse, it robbed you of any hope for success. It took you away from home, education, security, friends, and family. It was an unforgiving subculture. The friends you had in the rodeo world abandoned you as soon as you left. Rodeo burned more dreams than it kindled.

Almost midnight, I walked outside with Shauna into the parking lot. The place was deserted, and we watched her sisters and their mother drive away. She told me that the sisters loved to argue. I shouldn't take it too seriously. Anyway, she had cast her lot with rodeo and was dreaming about a new red 3500 Dodge Ram pickup to haul her barrel-racing horses. She was intent on a career in rodeo, even though her sisters were holding their breath about her decision. Rodeo was in her blood. But it was going to cost a ton of money.

Diana, Mickie's older sister, is a trim, athletic woman in her late forties, not a hair out of place, who insists that rodeo has nothing to do with the West; it is a sport. We met at her office and talked across a long conference table. Dressed in a tailored jacket and pants, she sat across from me and never showed any doubt about her judgments. As rodeo queen in the mid-1960s, her role was to promote the sport; she wasn't interested in what the rodeo might symbolize. And it certainly did not exist to preserve a connection to the rural West. "Most of your rodeo queens were not raised in a ranch setting. They were raised in a city setting and they do not know how to read a cow. Their horse does not know what a cow is." A rodeo queen had an exciting, promotional job to do, and she did it. It brought honor and respect, but it was also hard work. Your image had to reflect the rodeo at its best. "It was a highlight of my life. I rode all my life and it was something I wanted to do. To me it was like someone now being chosen Miss Junior Miss or Miss Washington. . . . It was just a big thrill." Like Bette, Diana wanted to be named Miss Rodeo Idaho. She had missed the crown by half a point.

By eighteen, Diana had spent hours in junior rodeo and gymkhanas, horse game competitions that test speed, agility, and endurance. She saw herself as a competitive horsewoman, but her family never wanted her to risk her body on rough rodeo sports. Riding horses developed physical fitness and promoted self-discipline. Today she was still an accomplished horsewoman, reining, riding, and exploring the canyons and creeks of northern Idaho and eastern Oregon.

With more money flowing in the national economy, the recreational horse culture of the 1960s boomed. Women started competing in local, state, and regional horse shows, saddle clubs, trail-riding associations, and cutting and reining competitions. Women were becoming visible again as rodeo cowgirls. Founded in 1948, the Girls Rodeo Association (the GRA—renamed the Women's Professional Rodeo Association [WPRA] in 1982) picked up speed in the 1950s but really made historical gains in 1967, when it won a battle against the Professional Rodeo Cowboys Association (PRCA) and earned the right to include a women's barrel-racing competition in the National Finals Rodeo. Although there was the All-Women's rodeo circuit, young women were discouraged from riding bulls or broncs but were encouraged to perform in such events as pole bending, goat tying, and the increasingly popular barrel racing.

Barrel racing is a horse-racing event for women in rodeo that goes back to the early twentieth century. To compete, women riders follow a clover-leaf course around three barrels. At breakneck speed, their horse must twirl around the barrels without losing precious seconds, then race across the finish line. One run lasts about sixteen to eighteen seconds. The rodeo historian Mary Lou LeCompte writes that the GRA wanted barrel racing to become a legitimate timed event in major rodeos as far back as the early 1950s. In 1950, the Houston Fat Stock Show and Rodeo included the event, but its media coverage was a pale second to Roy Rogers, Dale Evans, and the sixty-seven women who were trying out for rodeo queen. LeCompte suggests that women barrel racers knew little about the successes of rodeo cowgirls before World War II. They didn't know about Prairie Rose Henderson, Mabel Strickland, or Bertha Blancett.

Only perseverance worked. By the 1960s, barrel racing had become a legitimate way for women to compete in the professional rodeo arena. But it was not until Title IX of the Educational Amendments was passed in 1972, banning sexual discrimination in schools for both academics and athletics, that a new era for women in sports began. Still, big strides in the financial success of rodeo

cowgirls would have to wait until 1980, when the Women's Professional Rodeo Association insisted that women have prizes equal to
men in the rodeo arena. The National Finals Rodeo resisted the
change in status for women. The WPRA won the battle of equal
prize moneys in the national finals only with financial backing
from Purina Mills in 1985. Charmayne James Rodman ruled the
barrel-racing world between 1984 and 1993, winning more money
in 1987 than any rodeo athlete, male or female.

Still, barrel racing made only partial inroads in a male-
dominated sport. And despite the money, I have often heard dis-
paraging remarks about "barrel bitches" cutting in where they
don't belong.

Maybe it was about hair after all. With women in the rodeo
arena, rodeo queens grew even longer curls. This was around the
time that the television series *Charlie's Angels* grew popular, with
its three female stars all decked out in guns, lip gloss, and extreme
hairdos. The Angels were sexy, they fought back, and no one
would mistake them for guys. The long straight hair for men and
women in the androgynous 1960s was officially over. Farrah Fawcett's glamorous locks sent thousands to the drugstore for perms,
gel mousse, and curling irons.

One queen told me that her daddy refused to let her cut her
hair. And he wanted it curled. She agreed. Long blond locks kept
that gender line utterly clear.

Even though rodeo strained under the social, political, and gender conflicts of the 1960s and 1970s and cowboys lost their luster
on the national stage, many locals held on fast with corporate help.
Rodeo queens kept the show going with a new job description.
They got briefcases, sponsors, barrel racing, hair spray, and glitter.
Sure, they were burdened with bills and responsibilities, but they
had more hair, clothes, tiaras, and horse-trailer rides. Only one

rodeo in the Northwest region resisted the trend. The Pendleton Round-Up insisted that its rodeo royalty appear only in pageboy cuts, even if it meant wearing a wig to hide the teased hair or massive perms. Bouffant hairstyles beware.

10

A Perfect Image

D o you want the truth or do you want lies?" Lee Ann, a 1993 rodeo princess, sat directly across from me at the bare table in the community center. She stared at me and did not look away. Her brown hair, worn long and straight, framed her calm, serious mouth. She spoke in a subdued and deliberate voice. She told me she knew what she was supposed to tell me about the rodeo, but she didn't want to talk about that.

Sure, there had been good things. She had even enjoyed herself sometimes, but she was burned out. It was exhausting to be "superpolite" and "superhappy" for a whole year. In fact, life as royalty was hell. The rodeo board, the chaperones, the businesses and corporations sponsoring the rodeo—all of them wanted a perfect image. Lee Ann was not perfect. She sat back in her chair, crossed her arms over her chest, and fluttered her purple fingernails. "No one is going to change me."

Doing her duty as a rodeo queen wasn't about putting on a good face; it was about turning Lee Ann into a person she could never be and would never want to be. "I was the rebellious one,"

Lee Ann explained. First there was the problem with her hair. "Whenever we went to a function, I had to curl it." Lee Ann would go through bottles of hair spray every week, taking up to four hours at one sitting to produce the mounds of curls required for her perfect image. "It fried my hair," Lee Ann complained. Her hair just didn't want to do what was required and neither did her personality. Anytime she was in public, she had to dress the part, and since the promotion of the rodeo had expanded to thirty-two weekends a year, she felt that she had lived in her cowboy gear for a full year.

It had all come to a head when she decided to dye a strand of her hair purple. Since the purple strand would be tucked under her cowboy hat at all public occasions, the act was one of private rebellion. No one knew except her friends and the chaperone. (Chaperones had became more common during the 1950s, and by the time Lee Ann was named princess in 1993, they were permanent fixtures on the rodeo road, acting as stand-in parents and shepherding the rodeo court through its maze of duties and complex clothing changes. They were usually volunteers, friends of rodeo board members or previous rodeo queens. And they could act as moral watchdogs.) Lee Ann's story leaked quickly. The purple strand sent tidal waves through the rodeo board, and Lee Ann was threatened with dismissal. It didn't matter that no one in the public would know. The board knew, and it did not approve.

Purple meant controversy. The color was adopted by alternative kids, dropouts, punk music, lesbians, and the drug culture. Purple gave the wrong signals. It was completely incompatible with the image of a rodeo queen or the image of a corporate icon sponsoring the rodeo. Lee Ann's small act of defiance set in motion a struggle over how much power she had and how far she could alter or resist what the adults in her rodeo world wanted.

The "perfect little image" that annoyed Lee Ann so deeply had also seduced her. Lee Ann loved the way the queen and her court looked when they were all dressed up. They shone like a string of rhinestones. She thought the long, curled hair looked fantastic with cowboy hats, and the glamour and beauty of the show-biz rodeo queen was still with her as she talked. After all, "all little kids look up to royalty," and many parents in town wanted their little girls to be queens. Hadn't her mother and grandmother? She would never have tried out if she hadn't had the rodeo queen bug herself. She only balked when the board asked so much from her that nothing of the real her was left.

Lee Ann was also blunt about the money. "It's very, very expensive. If you don't have money, there's no point in trying out." You had to have the backing of your family, and not just your parents but aunts, uncles, cousins, and friends, too. Sometimes ten to fifteen people would be involved in getting the queen ready for a parade or grand entry. You needed backing. Lee Ann felt that her grandmother had practically taken the full year off to support her in the effort.

The previous year, Lee Ann had been rodeo queen at Grangeville Border Days and had had a great time. A town of only a few thousand people, Grangeville ran a rodeo that spent way less money. She felt close to the town. The people in the community weren't looking at her all the time, sizing her up. It was a completely different experience from the year on the rodeo court at Lewiston's larger, professional rodeo. There she had lost herself, and she was still mad.

Someone had turned up the volume on rodeo frustration. Talking with women who were queens in the 1980s and 1990s, I heard a high-pitched resentment against the professional rodeo circuit. The complaints came from opposing camps. Some resented the"perfect image" they were forced to adopt, and others embraced that same perfection all the more. The disappointments were deeper, the expectations higher. The tensions could explode, especially in a small town.

Several months after meeting Lee Ann, I was visiting Joseph, Oregon, near the Eagle Cap Wilderness Area. I went to watch rodeo queen tryouts at the local fairgrounds. The rodeo stands were sprinkled with small groups of women and some families. I trudged up the stairs with my bag, packed with camera, tape recorder, and notebooks. I was looking for my contact and finally found her, a short woman with dark brown hair and a welcoming smile.

Jeanine was sitting near the previous year's rodeo court. These girls would hand over the crown to the newly appointed court. The three young women huddled next to each other two rows above where Jeanine sat barely looked up when I greeted them. Jeanine introduced me. There was not a smile among them. Jeanine frowned at them and sat down beside me to explain quickly how the tryouts worked. Three women had already been selected to be on the court, but the queen still needed to be chosen from among them. Horsemanship, speaking ability, poise, and ticket sales all went into the selection. In a few minutes, the three new court members would ride a preset Western equitation pattern as part of the final selection process. Jeanine looked weary; she was relieved when I assured her I could take care of myself while she worked. She rushed away.

I tried to make conversation with the previous court. One girl smiled vaguely when I said they must be glad they didn't have to go through tryouts again. They seemed remarkably bored by the whole thing. Later, at the rodeo court dinner, I heard that the sullen court had been a handful for the rodeo committee and the chaperones. They were disagreeable and wouldn't do anything they were told. After dinner, the three hung out with their boyfriends, flaunting their skinny, tight-jeaned dates like trophies. They definitely had a teenage attitude, and it did not go down well with the adults in the room. All eyes were on the next year's court. Would these new girls bring the sparkle back to this small Western town?

I could not help but think about the 1991 movie *My Heroes Have Always Been Cowboys*. The adolescent son of one character is a rebellious teenager who wears baggy jeans and an earring. He is withdrawn, sullen, alienated. By the end of the movie, he has learned the rodeo cowboy way, has lost his earring, wears cowboy jeans and a hat, and hangs out with the men in his newly adopted family. He has been transformed into a God-fearing, family-loving man.

The queen and her court were supposed to live an all-American lifestyle. They were supposed to uphold traditional values in an increasingly hostile, decadent world. As one mother said about the desire to be a rodeo queen, "There aren't a lot of dreams out there. It's a wholesome dream." To some, rodeo had become a way to offset the corruption of America and its fall from traditional Christian principles. The rhetoric was thick and uncomplicated.

During the 1980s and 1990s, a wave of what some historians have called "plain-folks Americanism" washed over the Western United States in reaction to the social changes of the 1960s and 1970s. A new pride in whiteness was edged with the defiant attitude of a victim. Resentments ran high about the favors showered on minorities and the obstacles put in the way of the white lower and middle classes. Religious fundamentalism gripped the West, reaffirming traditional family values and allegiance to God and country. By the 1980s, the frontier myth of a simpler time when hard work by white settlers prevailed to build a great nation played well in the rural West and in the Oval Office. Ronald Reagan and the rise of the new right galvanized the political and moral emotions of many people living in the rural West. At his Western White House, Rancho del Cielo, nestled above Santa Barbara, Reagan sank fence posts and joked about his youth in a happier America.

Rodeo circles embraced older populist beliefs, mixing them with fundamentalist Christian values. White rodeo queens would keep the borders between the outside corrupt world and the all-American inner circle clear. They were representatives of a renewed commitment to family, God, and country. They were perfect, lily-white, all-American girls.

The problems arose when the queens did not follow the social script. The members of the previous court had failed in this mission. They just didn't seem like good country people with clean moral values. Sadly, the next year's court would break the hearts of the town.

Erica, Bridget, and Katie thought of themselves as the "three musketeers," that is, until Katie turned their rodeo fantasy upside down and resigned from the court in midseason. Right before the hometown rodeo in July, she quit and left Erica and Bridget scrambling to make the event look normal.

I had first met Katie at the rodeo queen tryouts. She rode a beautiful paint horse and carried herself with grace and confidence. Rodeo queen material for sure, I thought, and I had picked her for the queen with Erica and Bridget as princesses. When I introduced myself during the tryouts, she seemed shy and didn't give me a happy, rodeo queen smile. In fact, she didn't smile much during the entire competition. By the end of that day, she and Bridget were chosen as princesses. Erica would be the queen.

As the rodeo season progressed, I hung around with the three young women at a number of parades in the area and spent time with them when they were getting their horses ready or eating on the rush. They wore classic Western clothes, slim black pants with deep-beige Western shirts and graceful cowboy hats. Their long curly hair was pulled back behind their ears and trailed down their backs. They worked hard training their horses, making certain everything was ready for each rodeo event. Their chaperone was kind and flexible. She really cared for these young women.

But something had gone wrong. After the rodeo season was over, I returned to Joseph to talk with Erica and Bridget. Since I had watched them over the season, I wanted to hear their impressions of their royalty reign. I wondered how they felt about what they had done.

I knew Katie would not be joining us. And I did not know what had happened at the end of the rodeo season. I met Erica and Bridget at a local restaurant, where we sat outside on a picnic bench talking. They had brought their scrapbooks for me to look at, and the pages were jammed with photos, newspaper clippings, letters, and cards. When I opened Bridget's scrapbook, the inside cover was dedicated to Katie, her photo was framed by the words "In Memoriam."

I was not prepared for the news. One night, soon after she had quit the rodeo, Katie had died in a car accident. Erica and Bridget wore their royalty outfits to the memorial service. They were still trying to make sense of what had happened. They both knew that if they had convinced Katie to remain a princess, she would have been with them at a rodeo instead of in that car the night of the accident.

During the conversation, Erica and Bridget told me about Katie's frustrations on the rodeo court and why they thought she had resigned. She didn't want to be a "Barbie doll." She was fed up with the expectations. Her father had wanted her to be rodeo queen since she was born—in fact, he had asked a former queen to help raise Katie as a rodeo queen. Katie was born into it, and now she was dead.

Both Bridget and Erica were distressed about the expectations people had heaped on Katie. The pressure from the community was too high. Their young voices carried the weight of this tragedy. They told me how they had talked about their frustrations with the Chamber of Commerce, the rodeo board, and many well-meaning rodeo supporters. They were looking to the adults for ways to make sense of what had happened. But they were still sorting out their sadness and confusion.

One of the conflicts between the rodeo board and Katie had been school. Katie had dropped out of the regular high school and had enrolled in an alternative school, but there was ambiguity about her status as a full-time student. In reaction, the rodeo board had quickly written a new provision that a rodeo queen must be a full-time student. They wanted to make sure they didn't have any problems in the future. Then Katie just quit.

Bridget and Erica's rodeo dreams had crashed with the loss of Katie's life. Bridget was trying to pick up some pieces. She was donating one of her horses to a summer horse camp that Katie's mother was putting together. The camp had been a long-term dream for Katie and her mother, and Bridget wanted to see it become a reality.

Other dreams were dissolving when I talked with Bridget and Erica after Katie's death and at the end of the Chief Joseph rodeo season. Erica had wanted to go on to try out for the Pendleton Round-Up rodeo court and the state rodeo queen competition, but she had been discouraged by an influential person in town who felt she didn't have the proper history. Transplanted from the urban corridor of the I-5 West, Erica's family was not one of the older families in town, and she did not have deep roots in the rural West. She was still a newcomer to some people in town. Erica was also told that her family was simply "not visible enough." This translated into a pretty thin code for not having enough money.

The rodeo simply cost too much. Erica was angry that there were clear limits to her future as rodeo queen. The final blow came when she and Bridget were excluded from a traditional saddle club associated with the rodeo.

I had to admit that I was losing my bearings talking to these young women. The rodeo boards demanded that these women perform as corporate icons, moral beacons, and pretty Barbie dolls. It all seemed too much. How had rodeo become so serious? How could these young people withstand the pressures?

Historian Richard White argues that statistics can help us to understand the negative power of the West as an imagined space. The rural West persists in our cultural imagination as wide-open spaces that promise fresh opportunities, second chances, and a new life. White notes that the reality was much grimmer. In the 1980s, young people living in the rural West were more violent than their ghetto peers. Yet the violence found in the rural West did not hold the media spotlight. But why not?

Domestic violence rates in the rural West are staggeringly high. Alcoholism, unemployment, cultural illiteracy, and poor standards of health rose in many small Western towns throughout the 1980s and 1990s. The suburbanization of the West into ranchettes and new mega-homesteads of the rich only made the problems worse.

Young people from small towns, ranches, and farms drifted to cities such as Spokane, Salt Lake City, and Boise to find jobs or to enlist in the military. Those lucky enough to have computer skills had a chance to survive with Internet jobs, but most had to settle for poor-paying service jobs. Economic expectations were low, and rural space became stifling, claustrophobic, worthy of the fiction of Raymond Carver and Annie Proulx, rather than Edna Ferber and Willa Cather. The liberating spaces of Cather's sunflowered prairies were reduced to the cramped interiors of trailers and the oppressive acres of Carver or Proulx.

In this context, nostalgia became defiant. Nostalgia originally referred to a sense of melancholy caused by prolonged absence from home. But nostalgia in the West involves the celebration of an imaginary home of Western tradition, rugged individualism, and infinite promise. Historically, that home never existed. Nostalgia became a substitute for facing and solving the hurtful and complex realities of home.

We know from historians that rodeo attendance declined throughout the 1960s and 1970s, so much so that promoters and stock contractors were worried that the end of the rodeo era might be in sight. But as one old cowboy and rodeo promoter told me, *Urban Cowboy*, released in 1980, spread Western fever back through the working class. At the same time, Ronald Reagan successfully packaged himself as a cowboy, riding his horse around Rancho del Cielo, having photos taken of himself splitting wood, and redecorating the Oval Office in avocado green and Frederick Remington bronzes of lone cowboys and Indians. The West had returned with a rejuvenated conservative mandate appealing to conservative working-class and middle-class values.

A quick look at the plot of *Urban Cowboy* shows how invented and abstract the Western way had become. In the movie, the rodeo world takes place against the backdrop of a monumental urban industrial plant. John Travolta plays a young hard hat who leaves his family behind in rural Texas and heads off to Houston. His uncle, a former rodeo cowboy, teaches him the necessary rodeo skills to take on the mechanical bull at a bar called Gilley's. His uncle's life is severed from the ranch. Not only has he preceded Travolta in looking for work in the city, but he also eventually dies in an industrial accident at the plant where they both worked. After his death, Travolta becomes obsessed with gaining glory on Gilley's mechanical bull.

The movie builds to a standoff between Travolta and Scott Glenn, who has taken up with Travolta's wife. A real rodeo cowboy, Glenn learned to ride bulls in prison. His rodeo is a harsh world of punishment, pain, and controlled violence.

(The journalist Daniel Bergner writes about prison rodeo in Louisiana as a rite of redemption. The brutal injuries the prisoners endure from bulls and horses somehow redeem them in the eyes of the spectators. Up to 5,000 locals and tourists lured by prison advertising came to see the show Bergner describes. Bergner admits that some spectators clap when prisoners are hurt, even severely hurt; but when their ride is glorious, the prisoners triumph. They act with bravery and courage in the face of danger and injury. The rodeo arena plays out a strange moral drama. It supposedly expiates sins, renews the soul, and allows the prisoners to reclaim their basic humanity.)

In *Urban Cowboy*, Glenn is not redeemed but is instead hardened by his prison experiences. Eventually, Travolta wins the bar competition against Glenn and gets his wife back. True love prevails, and the bad guy goes back to jail.

In the movie, the men are desperate for jobs at the plant even if it means they might die on the line. They have no interest in returning to the farm or ranch life of their parents or grandparents. The dream of the ranch is dead and buried. Night entertainment— booze, sex, and fake bulls—is the only place to dream the cowboy dream. So what if the bull is mechanical and does not shit, stomp, or gore? The clothes are the same, the music rocks, and the dance of the cowboy, hand raised, heels flying, hips and back twisted in a grotesque parody of control, releases the working man from drudgery and guarantees him glory. He is an imitation rodeo cowboy performing before a crowd of working-class peers.

Women are not rodeo queens in this world but mainly voyeurs who gaze at the men in their tight jeans and flashy shirts. Urban cowboys are erotic fantasies for wealthy women who collect them like shiny trinkets for fun in bed. To spite his wife, Travolta takes up with a high-class woman who went slumming, picking up cowboys to antagonize her CEO father. To her, a real man does not wear a three-piece suit; a real man wears a string tie, boots, a belt buckle, and a hat angled over his eyes. The rodeo cowboy as whore, the rodeo cowboy as fool.

Country Western music also made a huge comeback in the 1980s and 1990s, controlling radio stations in many areas of the United States, and rodeo attendance fed off the same audience. Music stars, not Western movie or television celebrities, became the new way to promote attendance at rodeos. In a backlash against the excesses of the 1960s and 1970s, the music of Country Western singers championed family values and rodeo cowboy heroes. Even though "beatin' and cheatin'" were still dominant themes, singers such as Alan Jackson, Randy Travis, and Amy Grant renewed the moral high ground of Country Western values.

The religious and political right filtered into both the music world and the world of rodeo. Rodeos were preceded by Christian prayer breakfasts, associations for Christian cowboys and cowgirls emerged, and many rodeos offered Christian services on the Sunday morning before the rodeo started, sometimes featuring the rodeo clown as minister. Called the Cowboy Church, this religious revival was dressed in the language of the pastoral West. Hymns were sung to the rhythms of Western music, and the congregations were dressed in Western wear. The lessons, taken from Christian fundamentalism, promoted a clear-cut set of conservative social behaviors.

One hot, dry Sunday morning at a rodeo, I attended Cowboy Church. The early morning crowd was thin, but eager. Sweet country music drew handfuls of people to the bandstand. Christian prayer meetings had been a part of this rodeo ground for almost twenty years, and the bleachers filled up quietly and slowly. In a tent nearby, free coffee and cookies sat next to booklets of rodeo cowboy testimonials in English and Spanish. "Jesus loves you . . . take it into your heart," sang the congregation. A woman in her fifties, dressed in a simple cotton dress, her hair falling in soft ringlets around her face, welcomed strangers into the open-air church next to the rodeo grounds. She leaned into the microphone, softly fingering the melody on her guitar.

Early morning sun pounded down on the members of the small congregation as they mixed rodeo and religion, the love of Christ and cowboys. Testimonials spoke to how individual lives had known the "slime pit of life" and received the forgiveness of the Lord. This love and forgiveness was the key to changing yourself, your family, friends, even the world. Its power was infinite.

Thanks were given to the community volunteers and the young people who manned the church booth, distributing pamphlets and Bibles. The community had taken a stand, holding up the rodeo cowboy for Christ as a means to make visible the way of the Lord. Biblical quotes spilled from the lips of the congregation. Bronc riders witnessed the moment that Christ entered their life. Team ropers struggled to understand how Christ's message could change their life. Mounted horsemen for God, they fought Satan and sin just as they faced their fear in the arena. The rodeo was a sanctified stage for the battle between good and evil, a place to understand salvation and experience redemption.

It was "just like magic," said Sara Jane. She had been a rodeo queen in 1991, and she still glowed from the experience. Sara Jane had too much energy for her small body. She could hardly sit still in the seat across from me at lunch. Blond curls set off her nervous face. The restaurant of the hotel where we met was so packed with heavy furniture that I felt like I was on a stage set for giants. Even the vinyl seemed extra thick. The room oozed Western excess. It was suffocating.

Sara Jane didn't seem to notice. She wanted to travel back fast to those glory days, and talking to me might make the ride quicker. The year Sara Jane had spent promoting the rodeo was like walking on a cloud. Five years later, she was still trying to relive the thrill, but she was stuck in the pain. When it was over, she felt "worthless as an empty can rolling down the street." The ride had ended too abruptly. As one rodeo board member had reminded many rodeo queen candidates, "There is no future in being a rodeo queen."

Some women in the 1990s don't see it that way. They see the rodeo queen experience as a stepping stone into a potential career, going from local to regional, state, and national competitions, and finally into one of the many corporations associated with rodeo, particularly Western-wear companies. But of all the women I talked with, only one had specifically benefited with a well-paid job from a corporate sponsor.

Sara Jane talked about how she "chose" to become a "product of the rodeo association" and to inject herself into the mold of what the rodeo wanted. The rodeo association wanted their rodeo queen to be a "product that can produce results" and to be "manageable." The rodeo queen had to take responsibility to sell the product. Her behavior had to set the right image to correspond with the product. Even though these expectations demanded that she control herself—not only her behavior, but her weight and the way she looked—they were worth it to Sara Jane.

A rodeo queen had to struggle with herself. For Sara Jane, that internal battle was necessary to win. There was a difficult "competition with self to make you the best product you can be." Sara Jane admitted there was no pay for this intensive work, but there was a payoff: You were recognized, loved, and accepted by the community. You had a sense of security and belonging. In the community, you were always the rodeo queen. "You keep having to live the dream for them," Sara Jane explained. She gave people "something to believe in." In her town and among her friends, everyone wanted to be a cowgirl or a cowboy. It was the dream that never dies.

I was having a hard time listening to Sara Jane. She was still drunk on rodeo glory, but I felt sad and depressed when she insisted that the rodeo was a place to "show the essence" of herself and in the next breath whispered that a part of herself disappeared when she traveled down the rodeo road. What did it mean to Sara Jane to see herself as a "product"? How was she different from the toothpaste and household detergents that dance across our TV screens, promising us better lives if we would only buy them? What happens when people become products? Do they dance and smile, too, chanting corporate jingles and offering a perfect world? For Sara Jane to become a product, she had to mold herself to management wishes. She had to empty herself, rearrange her bits and pieces to construct a perfect image.

There was a layer of urgency in Sara Jane's voice. Her desire to be a perfect rodeo product had a missionary side. She was selling the Western way of life. Sara Jane felt that government policies, environmentalism, the urbanization of agricultural lands, and general decadence had all conspired to ruin the pastoral vision of the rural Western dream. The tenacity of the rodeo cowboys, cowgirls, stock contractors, local boards, corporate sponsors, and queens defied these threats. The rodeo queen was there to shout, "We are still here," to fight back urban nightmares and suburban greed.

Sara Jane yearned to be accepted by the local rodeo community. The rodeo world became the place for her to feel a sense of continuity and meaning. If she failed to receive the recognition of her community, it was because she had not worked hard enough to manage herself. She admitted the constant vigilance needed to perform the role of rodeo queen perfectly. She had to scrutinize herself to keep the right weight, hairstyle, and skin tone for the job of rodeo queen. She had to work without doubt. She had to pump herself up for the job. She had to be perfect.

As a result, she was accepted by those in the community who valued the rodeo culture, but not everyone did. Many left town on the weekend of the rodeo because they didn't like the crowds, the noise, and all the hype. To them, the rodeo didn't seem like a community celebration anymore. Instead, it was a nuisance. Sara Jane felt the backlash against "buckle bunnies." Respect was a problem. Nobody understood the rules anymore.

This same urgency hit me hard when I met a young woman who had just finished her year as a rodeo queen and was headed for the state competition. She wanted to sparkle, to sparkle, to sparkle. I kept hearing the phrase in my mind as she talked. Tami had always wanted to be a rodeo queen. As a young girl, she would gaze at the court riding downtown in the parade, a vision of total glamour. Now she sat in her spacious living room on a steep hill overlooking the Snake River. Her father owned the sporting-goods store in town, and they had a beautiful small-acreage ranchette on the outskirts of town.

Her voice had a lilting Western twang, like a Country Western singer. There was an enormous portrait of her in the entryway. She stood, dressed in a buckskin fringed dress, her hands delicately touching each other in front of her. Her face was topped by an enormous white cowboy hat. Mounds of blond curls fanned away from the hat's brim. Her daddy never wanted her to cut her hair, and she never did. Even though her hair was naturally bone straight, she loved the curls.

It took me a few minutes to get my bearings. Maybe it was the smile and the voice. Maybe it was the aura of perfection that Tami conveyed—a loving family, a totally supportive community, and a worldview that was so positive I started to feel disoriented. I felt I was in the presence of a young woman who lived and breathed the rodeo party line. Not a single word would come out of her mouth to indicate in any way that the rodeo, the community, and she and her family were not inhabiting the sweetest, most perfect happy-land of the new West. I had entered the world of roboqueens.

Nothing, absolutely nothing, bad would be said about anything. Tami's favorite movie was *Eight Seconds*. Released in 1994, this film told the story of a real life bull rider, Lane Frost, who became a rodeo hero after a fatal goring from a bull at Cheyenne Frontier Days in 1989. Presented as a pseudo-documentary, the film follows Lane's determination to bull ride, his rocky marriage to a barrel racer, his reconciliation with his wife, and his sudden death riding Red Rock, a magnificent bull who threw every cowboy. To Tami, the movie was God's truth about the West, and rodeo represented the best of America.

Rodeo preserved Western heritage for her generation and those to follow. Events in the rodeo from bull riding to roping a calf gave the audience a window into the world America was and should be again. When I asked her directly what Western heritage meant to her, she came to a temporary halt, then launched into a discussion of "getting back to our roots and what our ancestors worked on perfecting." Somehow the "spirit of the West" must continue on through the rodeo, giving people a sense of "what it was before it was rodeo."

The vagueness of her responses, and their slippery feel, made me wonder whether there were any specific values or morals related to the role of rodeo queen. I asked her what she thought. "I have very high standards, and I wanted basically to impose them on other people to actually let them know that this is great and this is okay and this is what kind of person you can be if you lead this way of life and have these high morals and standards," Tami answered. Tami felt that she was a means to preserve the best of America. She wanted everyone to be held to the same high moral standards, whether they were rodeo queens, stock contractors, or rodeo performers. When I pushed, Tami had a difficult time giving a specific example of what she meant by high morals and standards. In fact, she said, "Golly."

My newfound cynicism over the moral mandates of the rodeo was only encouraged when I visited a small local rodeo at the beginning of the season in April to watch the rodeo queens in the parade and bust-out. I had decided to bring my camera down to the front of the stands and take some photos over the fencing that cut me off from the rodeo arena. The rodeo in Asotin had been tough on the participants, and young men were scattered on the ground around the Emergency Medical Services truck. Several rodeo cowboys had become hung up in their hand ropes, flopping like Raggedy Andys off the sides of the bulls. It had been painful to watch.

I wanted to get some photos of local women participating in a special event titled "Mutton Dressing." No rodeo I had ever attended had such an event, and I wasn't quite sure what to expect. But after watching all those men get pounded, I guess I was ready for a break.

I should have known something was amiss when a man working the gate grabbed me and pushed me into the arena, saying it would be easier for me to take my pictures from inside. I heard the announcer bellow out in a loud voice, "The women dress them, the men undress them." Then at least twenty women in teams of three or four burst into the arena. A few seconds later, a group of about ten or fifteen sheep were released into the arena. The sheep flew around, leaping in the air and trying to scramble away as fast as they could. The women charged and tried to hold onto a sheep, wrestle it to the ground, and then dress it in bonnet, bra, and panty hose.

The crowd roared with belly laughter. The sound was deafening. There was so much dust and pandemonium that for a few seconds, I stood still in disbelief as women scrambled under sheep trying desperately to pull panty hose down their kicking and wiggling legs. One woman was completely under a sheep and covered in dirt as she tried to hold the swirling mass of wool still long enough for her friends to tie the bonnet around its shaking head. I started to take pictures but quickly put the camera aside and watched. One sheep was stunned and lay frozen, its head covered by a crooked bonnet.

Rodeo is filled with jokes about bestiality, men's penises and balls. Some rodeo announcers have a reputation for their foul mouths. In their attempt to make rodeo a family event, some communities have stayed away from announcers who play up the sexual innuendoes and jokes. In this case, the announcer was having a good time with the mutton dressing, especially its painfully obvious sexual overtones.

From my perspective, it looked like the women were raping and humiliating the sheep. The goal of the contest was to dress the sheep like a "lady"—to make the sheep submit to the costume of bonnet, bra, and pantyhose. The sheep were thrown down, tugged, pulled, and crushed before the clothes would go on. They looked ridiculous, dressed in their little hats and pathetic bras. Their legs were absurd, sticking out like trapped sticks thrusting around in pantyhose casings. In this same event one year later, the men would try and ride these dressed sheep, these women surrogates, and complete the sexual link between men, women, and animals visible to the howling crowd.

The rodeo queens sat in the bleachers and laughed loud and long with everyone else at the farce perpetuated on the sheep. Their howling stripped away the veneer of rodeo morality. Covered with dust, I left the arena. I sat outside on the dirty white bleachers trying to figure out what the hell rodeo meant to all these hysterical fans. Where had all the moral righteousness gone, the Christian crusade, the ideal virgin queens? The weight of Christian morality, corporate iconography, and rodeo queen perfection crashed down amid the bleating of those sheep, struggling to get away.

Dreaming Las Vegas

The giant Coca-Cola bottle stood elegantly at the edge of the pavement, a crystal monolith turned elevator welcoming me to Las Vegas. Workmen in white toxin-repelling suits brushed the final coats of resin on a miniature replica of "New York, New York." Since my last visit in the fall of 1997, the architectural grandeur of Paris, Venice, and Bellagio has risen out of the desert floor. That morning, the serene head of the MGM lion watched Manhattan emerge into the clean desert air. The vibrancy of the early light exaggerated the inversions of scale. Things I was used to holding in my hand as a child towered over me. A metropolis was shrunk to one city block. Grandeur downsized; the banal made colossal. The arrogance was invigorating. Las Vegas was an adult playground where the familiar icons of America became toys and decorations for a game of chance.

I had come to Las Vegas to watch the tryouts for the Miss Rodeo America pageant, held annually right before the National Finals Rodeo. The Flamingo Hilton Hotel glowed in pink, and a banner welcoming the MRA contestants reassured me that I was indeed in the right place. I hadn't seen anyone looking remotely like a cowboy, let alone a potential Miss Rodeo America, but the weeklong schedule of luncheons, interviews, speeches, and fashion shows plastered by the registration counter betrayed an entire world of rodeo glamour hiding in the bowels of the casino-hotel.

After checking in, I was led to a hotel room looking out on Caesar's Palace, a faux Italian villa, frosted with fountains and blue spotlights guiding limousines and weary travelers into its cavernous playrooms. I dumped my bags and wandered back out to the Caesar's Palace shopping mall, where I listened to the cyborg sculptures retelling Roman myths. Clearly, anything could happen in this town.

But how could I be prepared for the neon pageantry of Miss Rodeo America? The pace was too fast, the message too strident. As I wandered around the Flamingo conference rooms, the rodeo mantra blasted at me again and again. Rodeo was not a mere sport but a belief in an American style of life, based on conservative Christian principles and family values. The setting was Las Vegas, but the message was pure country. I wandered around the slot machines, trying to make sense of what I was hearing, what I was being told by the young women pinning their hopes on seizing the prize, the middle-aged women who keep the music going, and the corporate sponsors who pinned dollar amounts on the values of the rodeo.

Like the rest of Las Vegas, the rodeo's sense of scale had altered. Suddenly, rodeo not only reflected Western heritage, it protected and preserved Western heritage. Its mission was colossal. A big bubble of moral superiority hovered over the Miss Rodeo America competition. I read cowboy prayers, heard cowboy litanies at lunch, and listened to moral vitriol about how America was going down the toilet because of Asians, Mexicans, and lax government policies. Rodeo represented the heart of America and had the power to resist disturbing changes in the country. The contestants were frontline fighters in the mission to convert the nation to the cowboy way. The need to keep America pure was a murmur underneath the Miss Rodeo America pageant. It popped up in speeches, events, and corporate sponsorships. Maybe it's working. On Saturday, January 20, 2001, Miss Rodeo America rode in George W. Bush's Inaugural Parade.

Even blue jeans seemed to be fighting in the war for the future of the nation. I was told that Wranglers had the right image. Wranglers didn't succumb to the sexual indulgence and gender bending of Calvin Klein or the endlessly adaptable market of Levis, which fit into urban ghettos, Israeli middle schools, and French cafés. Wranglers spelled pure all-American cowboy. Everything at the rodeo had to stand for something relating to the moral heart of America; jeans couldn't be mere products, a way to make money. There had to be a moral gloss. They could be sexy, but the women in them had to look and act cute. Local and corporate support was supposed to fit like a glove with the sermons about rodeo as a home for positive work ethics, honesty, and Christian family values. But the strain of excessive commercialism hit against the moral prattle of the sponsors.

I started to read Wrangler's ads as a moral code: "It takes a special brand to know the people that love this land and call it their own." How could a brand of jeans "know" the intimate relationship of love between a people and their land? Was this a secret code alerting the potential consumer to their right to call the land their own? Was this a play on the "love it or leave it" language of the 1960s and 1970s?

I couldn't shake the feeling that this moral language rested on the "you know what I mean" brand of ethics. We know what we mean because we don't need to explain ourselves to each other, and we sure as hell don't want to explain it to you because then we would have to declare openly our prejudices and beliefs. The language we share is clear and obvious to us. We aren't going to tell you what we mean because it would be misunderstood, or worse, it would be judged, evaluated, and rejected by all those outsiders who have taken over America. There was no room for debate. You are either in or out of this moral landscape, period. You either know what "family values" means as a code for a worldview or you are not included in the family.

The evangelical atmosphere promoted by the organizers and the corporate sponsors filtered down to the scrapbooks of the MRA contestants, their speeches, and conversations at lunch. Some scrapbook pages echoed familiar Christian sentiments. Several reproduced the Cowboy Prayer, asking the "Heavenly Father" for his blessing, not his favoritism: "We ask that you be with us at this Rodeo, and we pray that you will guide us in the Arena of Life. We don't ask for special favors; we don't ask not to draw a chute-fighting horse or never break a barrier. Nor do we ask for all daylight runs, or not to draw a steer that won't lay." Instead, the prayer asks for fair admission to a pastoral afterlife: "Help us Lord, to live our lives in such a manner that when we make that last inevitable ride to the country up there, where the grass grows lush, green and stirrup-high, and the water runs cool, clear and deep, that you as our Last Judge, will tell us that our entry fees are paid."

Other scrapbook pages were more strident and militaristic, advocating punishment for desecration of the American flag and exhibiting a defiant grassroots patriotism. The edge of threat against America came out loud and clear. In one scrapbook, the American flag had been painted and its stripes formed these words: "I shall never be possessed; I shall only be shared, remaining free forever. I am America."

Counter to this moral bravado was a queasy feeling floating around the pageant and the rodeo finals that America and Americans had left the sport behind. People were painfully aware that rodeo was losing its audience. From the Professional Rodeo Cowboys Association president down to the local sponsors, they debated how to win a larger share of the traditional American fan base—people who watched sports like baseball, football, and basketball—as well as the working-class audience that preferred demolition derbies, wrestling, car racing, and monster truck rallies.

Rodeo was struggling to stay in the money. On top of that, sponsors were besieged by hate mail from animal-rights activists. The sense of siege only heightened the belief that America had changed for the worse. Even some of the Las Vegas taxi drivers I talked with thought the rodeo crowd was in trouble. They did not like their attitude and the fact they did not have enough money to blow on tips. Rodeo people were economic losers, not the professional moneyed crowd of doctors, dentists, lawyers, and businessmen who made these cab drivers' day. Plus they were self-righteous. They were cut off, dreaming about the way things used to be, preaching too much, and pinching pennies to pay their bills.

What the taxicab drivers did not see was the money floating around the rodeo world. The most flagrant excess was in the wardrobes of the Miss Rodeo America candidates. A candidate for Miss Rodeo America spent at least $10,000 on clothing, and $15,000 or $20,000 would be even better. Parents had dug down deep in their pockets after tracking down every penny of sponsor support they could find. The money kept flowing like the din of coins in the casinos.

The rodeo meant mink jackets cut in Western style, hats with lavish feathered and snakeskin bands, elaborate dyed leatherwear worked with hand tools, and beaded or embroidered satin shirts. Many contestants had their clothes professionally designed, and those who couldn't afford it stood out painfully.

And the clothes were beautiful. Deep-emerald buckskin

embroidered with white silk threads and beadwork. Cream buckskin split skirts with hand-tooled flowers. Turquoise and silver belts, earrings, and bracelets. Rhinestones had vanished, replaced by silver and gold tiaras, studded with precious stones. Silk, satin, gabardine, and suede, the clothes of the state rodeo queens blended Western flash and traditional Native American handicrafts. Several of the leather outfits were works of art, and in another time and place might have ended up in a museum documenting the late twentieth-century's nostalgia for Western movie images and Native American material culture.

A few candidates still championed the homespun and the homemade in their geometrically cut shirts and skirts. They looked almost quaint next to their finished sisters, who had gone through modeling clinics, speech classes, and endless fittings for their weeklong wardrobes.

One man explained to me that his wife had taken everything in hand. She had always wanted a daughter, and now she had her dream: a rodeo queen candidate. He was grateful that his wife could put all her energy into perfecting the queen. A dress designer shaped the clothes elegantly to the young woman's long, slender body. A horse trainer helped her achieve a finished look. He was worried about her riding, though. His protégé was not quite there yet. She definitely needed more time with the horse. She hadn't grown up around horses, he explained, hoping I would understand. He thought she could get by if she only had more time with the horse. The clothes were easy. His wife knew clothes.

By the end of our talk, he was confident they could win. Their rodeo queen candidate always shone. She loved people and loved to smile. He told me about how she would come right over to you in a crowd of people and welcome you in. She wanted to make you feel at home even in the big city. She loved people, he repeated. He asked me, had I ever seen a warmer smile? He was proud. She was "deeply religious." She was the "perfect girl." She would make a perfect Miss Rodeo America.

Other parents were less enthused. They thought the deck was stacked against their daughters. Call it sour grapes, but they were certain that they or their daughters did not fulfill a not-so-hidden agenda. Maybe it was the investment in clothes, or coming from the right state, or having the right value system, or the correct tone of voice and smile, they weren't sure. But they did know that they were losers in a game of promotion that went way beyond what they had ever anticipated.

Of course, some of them simply came from the wrong corner of the country. What could Miss Pennsylvania or Miss Arkansas or Miss New Hampshire really have to say about the rodeo? How could she represent it? She couldn't, and she hadn't. Since its start in 1956, there had been only two winners from east of the Mississippi—one from Michigan, the other from Louisiana. The rest had been from the "real" West, mainly from the states of Texas, Idaho, Colorado, Utah, and Wyoming.

From what I could tell, only white women had ever become Miss Rodeo America. No one had cracked the color line. It wasn't their political beliefs that held candidates of color back. Certainly I had known American Indians with conservative Christian values and quite a few Chicanos and Asian Americans who had photos of Ronald Reagan and Newt Gingrich on their living-room walls. Native Americans, African Americans, and Mexican Americans participated in the rodeo world. Yet for forty-five years, the politics of representation had never been tested.

I wondered how long it would take. In several of the current presentations by individual contestants, Native Americans and Mexican vaqueros were being used as familiar stage props for retelling the history of the Old West. Miss Hawaii made a valiant effort to explain that she was a *happa*, claiming Hawaiian, Chinese, Portuguese, German, English, Irish, Swedish, Norwegian, and American Indian ancestry. Despite her history of ranching on the island of Molokai, she didn't have a chance. Her West was not the "real" West of American mass culture. No matter how much she talked them up, *paniolo* were not real cowboys. Even contestants from the real West had to remind everyone that they were cowgirls at heart and hadn't gone too far off into potatoes or oil.

Some parents and chaperones were there mainly to protect their candidates from the pageant. One chaperone had come fifteen years earlier as a candidate and had been so traumatized by the experience that she decided never to let anyone from her state come without mental, emotional, and financial preparation. The contest could flatten you, she said. One mother told me they would never do it again, and several others wanted to talk in private on the phone about how horrible the experience had been for themselves and their daughters.

One mother and daughter pair walked around like calm strangers in the midst of a carnival. The daughter was probably going to be a candidate the following year. They had been warned by friends to check the scene out first. Quiet, gentle people, they sat at the dinner and watched the parade of young women in plastic-coated jeans on the fashion runway jump and twirl, trying hard to make their dance look like something seen on MTV. The pair lived far out in the country, and we shouted over the loud music at dinner about horses and the problems they had pulling a recent foal. The mother was concerned that Jamie, her daughter, needed to find out what the world was about. It was the process that mattered to her, not the winning. Jamie needed exposure.

They knew it would be hard. They would have to call on old friends, appeal to rodeo queens around the state, and pool family funds to get Jamie here next year, but it would be worth the effort. Besides, Jamie knew how to win. She had been riding her barrel horse for years. She was not going to marry the first guy from her hometown who asked. She was going to find out about the world.

Jamie's mother was careful with her, protective. They walked around the casino and the luncheon ballrooms, never straying too far from each other. They kept talking about horses and the ranch. They kept wondering about how Dad was doing without them and what he would think about the scene at Las Vegas. As the week went by, I thought Jamie grew more confident and eager. Her mother seemed sadder, more watchful. She kept glancing nervously at her daughter. How could she protect her from the disappointment of the world?

At another event, I sat at a table and listened to a young woman from California who refused to let the event tarnish her dreams. She spoke fast, her familiar story going something like this: MRA is a career move. I can learn a lot here. I want to work in the corporate world, probably public relations. I really want a job like that dream job that Miss Rodeo America got a few years back, working in Western wear, becoming a corporate spokesperson. I like people, always have. A smile can tell a lot about a person. I have to believe in myself and believe in the product. I love the rodeo, always have. My mother helps me with the clothes. She has a friend who sews. We go over there and she is so nice to us. Her husband always comes into the living room where there are sequins and rhinestones everywhere and he always tells me how pretty I look. My mother doesn't mind. She loves to sew, too. Never had much to do with horses or rodeo, but she loves to sew.

Everybody was dreaming. They kept looking and hoping. Most were disappointed. A major speaker at one luncheon reminded the contestants to "learn from every opportunity" and "celebrate the rodeo." "We have not lost what made this sport so good," he said. He urged the girls "to be professional": "Talk it, walk it, act it." And he reassured them that thousands of women would want to change places with them if they won. Then again, he said, the "taste of defeat" has "a richness all its own."

⁎ ★ 𓃾 ⁎ ★

Exhausted from watching the competition, I wandered out into Las Vegas. I gravitated toward the art galleries since I thought they might provide some space, a small reference point, from which to look at the pageant.

In the little town of Joseph, Oregon, the art galleries burst with bronze sculptures of cowboys, horses, and Indians. Some of it is Western kitsch, but there is also strong, innovative work. In Las Vegas, the art galleries appeared like magic shows, blending Disney-style animation, New Age fantasy landscapes, and hyperrealism. There were several art galleries at the Caesar's Palace mall. They beckoned to me like a carnival freak show. The rooms glowed with violet and chartreuse airbrushed images, laser light shows, crystal-clear aquariums, and rococo romance. I keep trying to find a place where my eye could rest, but resting was not allowed. Acrylic paintings depicted blue dolphins cavorting with Mickey Mouse characters. Muscle-beach men paid tribute to Amazon women beneath a waterfall of crystal clarity. Every image swirled in a landscape of staged props, part cartoon, part utopia.

I stepped back into the dark cavernous mall interior, lit by the artifice of a Venetian evening sky, a welcome relief after the forced dazzle of the art galleries. A couple walked by me dressed like Anthony and Cleopatra, complete with an entourage of slaves. Their costumes jingled. Nothing here was real. There was no point in trying to unravel meanings. Japanese businessmen, Russian tourists, a group of American dentists, and smartly dressed Europeans ambled next to me underneath the faux sunsets of a fake Venice, listening to the words of Bacchus as he winked every hour on the hour, all day and all night. Even the meaning of time had slipped away.

Dazed but not undone, I returned to the pageant. I was tired. I wanted to get away. I wanted fresh air. I longed to follow the sun from its pale yellow rise to its deep red falling. I thirsted for simplicity and the sound of the wind. I counted the hours until Miss Rodeo America was crowned.

At the coronation, I sat at a table where everyone was in a bad mood. The parents were disgusted. Their faces screwed up as the finalists' names were announced. No surprises there. The contestants looked exhausted. What would happen if I walked out right now, one girl said, right now in the middle of this banquet? Do you think anyone would notice? Do you think anyone would care?

But the ritual was stronger than she was. The young woman sat glued to her chair waiting to hear who had won, to be confirmed in her suspicions that from the start she'd never had a chance. She knew that from the beginning. She was from the East Coast and her accent would not work as Miss Rodeo America. She did not have the look of a country girl gone glamorous. Her hair, her nails, her clothes were all like the winner's, but her voice, her gestures, her attitudes were wrong. Not Miss Rodeo America material. Here was living proof we needed more quality control in the state competitions, I was told by people long associated with the pageant. How do we get all those good country values from states like New Jersey? Where was the ranch land and the open, endless sky? Not at my table, not today. The parents sat fuming, wishing they had never come.

Their anger washed over the speeches floating from the finalists' mouths. Their words blended together in my mind: *My dream has come true. Come here and pose with me next to the people who*

made this possible, my mother and father, my trusty horse, my spon-
sors, the hundreds of people who made my clothes, fixed my hair,
taught me how to walk and stand, what to say and how to say it.
When not to talk is as important as talking, you know. I love people
and that is what this is all about, people and the love of rodeo. I
want everyone in the world to love rodeo. I want to bring rodeo to
every country in Asia, Africa, and South America. I want them to
feel the love a cowboy has for his horse and his family. I want them to
feel what it is like to hold on past when the hurting starts. I want
them to understand the rodeo cowboy way. I want them to under-
stand the beauty of the Indian way. I want them to know what the
West stands for and why it must be preserved no matter the cost, no
matter the pain.

The Last Rodeo

In 1935, the first rodeo queen of the Omak Stampede in Omak, Washington, was selected by the number of purchases made in her name at the local stores. A contestant gained 100 votes for every fifty cents spent. The townspeople voted with their pocketbooks, assigning their allotted votes to their favorite candidate. The *Omak Chronicle*, the local paper, registered the unbelievable success of linking the queen contest to the purchasing power of consumers. Quickly the sales mounted. The top four contestants counted over 400,000 votes.

By the end of the voting frenzy, the town could hardly believe that Bertha Robbins had won with 4,750,500 votes. The three runner-ups all hovered around the 3 million mark. Who would have guessed that the rodeo queen race could whip up such a buying spree in this small rural community? The rodeo had indeed come to town, and with it a Western formula, fusing cowboy glamour and promotional consumerism.

Reading the newspaper accounts of this 1930s rodeo queen contest, I enjoyed the easy equation of dollars and election. Voting and cash-register receipts were locked together without any feigned talk about morality, Western tradition, and patriotism. Simply add up the total figure of goods bought and crown the queen. A diamond ring and a silk dress were consolation prizes for the losers.

The rodeo was a relief for Omak. The town, set at the edge of the Confederated Colville Indian Reservation, was plagued by conflicts over Indian lands, the allotment system, the Wheeler-Howard bill, and the distribution of Conservation Corps jobs among Indians and whites. The rodeo festivity read like a quick fix. Thousands of fans were expected to pour into the community, bolstering the local economy. The Omak Department Store ran full-page ads of sleek fall hats next to bucking broncos. Dollar signs were everywhere.

How different Omak's rodeo was when I visited in 1998. Despite the development of orchards, logging, hunting, and the occasional cattle ranch, the economy never flourished in this region. The only place I saw dollar signs in abundance was at Grand Coulee Dam over fifty miles away. I walked over to the dam one night to see a lasershow. Neon-green dollars danced across the monumental walls of the dam while the hum of electricity from the monster power cables lining the steep, arid hillsides drowned out any hope of night silence. The money seemed to follow the cable lines straight out of the region as quickly as the crackling current.

In Omak, people struggled to get by, and the rodeo had remained a part of the promise of the Western utopia. In the 1990s, the rodeo was more than a money-making scheme; it had become a religion of sorts, a belief system with apostles. The rodeo talk was as thick as the mayo on the hamburgers at the local diner. Rodeo was all about national bravado, feel-good Americanism, and the Western way of life. Although not all the locals loved the rodeo, many people in town promoted the rodeo through videos, advertising, local books, and tourism junkets.

Sitting in the bleachers at the rodeo, I was asked once again to connect with the rural drama of "hard work and integrity." The announcer claimed that "cowboy spirit" infused every person "no matter where they lived" or how they made their living. I flashed on how many times in the last six years I had been told that the rodeo preserves "the good of the nation" and marks a "way of life" dedicated to family values, Western heritage, and the American dream, kept alive by the "true American cowboy."

I thought back on how I had felt four years earlier when I was visiting some rodeo royalty in eastern Oregon. The eighteen-year-old rodeo queen and her princess told me that rodeo people, including themselves, "hated Democrats, environmentalists, and gays." I was astonished that their political and social outlook could be reduced to such simple platitudes of hate. And why?

Cyra McFadden, the daughter of Cy Taillon, probably the most popular rodeo announcer of the twentieth century, whose silver voice dominated the professional rodeo arena, wrote about how her father was often compared to John Wayne and embodied the"shoot first, argue later" brand of Western values. Cy had become a symbol of political conservatism in the 1950s, and his daughter described how he worked hard to make rodeo respectable and acceptable as a professional sport. His voice made rodeo cowboys into heroes and the politics of the West into a battle cry of moral certitude.

The surprise to me was how political and moral the rodeo world still was fifty years later. Rodeo queens were often under pressure to keep alive a particular vision of the West. They needed to promote moral certitude and political conservatism. Dressed in buckskin skirts, cowboy hats, and embroidered Western shirts, they embodied Western values. They performed, in deadly earnest, stories about what it means to be a "true" American.

What I had witnessed over the previous six years confirmed my sense that in the late nineteenth century, the Wild West show and its successor, the rodeo, became pageants to represent national history. They were what some historians called mass-producing traditions, dramatizing the imagined deeds of a frontier and pioneer past. As such, they never showed us what had really happened. Instead, they glossed over the conflicts and contradictions in our national past. They propagated a seductive collective story of bravery, individualism, and success. They combined popular entertainment, consumerism, and nationalism to create what Benedict Anderson called an "imagined community."

That was why the rodeo in Omak could never rest on a simple commercial formula. The rodeo was also asked to represent the heart of America, its ranching past, its pioneering spirit, its cowboy way, its tenacious will, its ultimate glory. The cowboy was constructed as a culture hero in the late nineteenth century, edged on by the likes of Teddy Roosevelt, Owen Wister, and Buffalo Bill Cody. In that period of reactionary politics, national boosterism, and imperialism, the rodeo continued the cultural formula, reenacting the necessity of the cowboy way.

Rodeo queens lent class to the frontier pageantry. They sanctioned the story. The queens were and still are mainly white women whose symbolic purity and strength of purpose enforce the need for a heroic cowboy counterpart. Riding the perimeter of the arena, they mark out the territory in which men compete for glory. The more extreme their feminine performance, the more macho the men can appear. The queen and cowboy need each other to perform a particular kind of national drama that reassures the "people" of their strength, virility, and power.

What was striking at the end of this project was the gradual change in the meaning of rodeo to the women involved. The rodeo queens in the 1930s and 1940s had lived through experiences that tempered their rhetoric. They had seen the loss of ranches, the hardships of farming, the scarcity of wealth; and they knew the rodeo court was not the life they lived. The women in the 1950s were also clearer about the gender and race roles in rodeo that made it a commercial product for both small-town and national consumption. What changed over the second half of the twentieth century was the use of the rodeo as a script to bolster a particular form of Americanism. Rodeo rhetoric claimed the heart of the country and arranged a set of prescribed values as a cure for the social, political, and economic fissures in the nation. The West was codified into a set of slogans repeated compulsively and without reflection by the advertising and promotional organizations of the rodeo. The queens followed suit. If they resisted, they did so at their peril. Bitterness and anger would be their reward.

Early on in this project, a Lewiston Roundup committee member put it this way: Rodeo was "the mirror image of an invented reality." Even I, who like to play with words and hardly ever believe in the closeness of what many people refer to as "the real," found this description daunting. The rodeo mirrored not reality but human inventions about reality. I had entered a cultural fun house. I couldn't look for the Old West in the rodeo. The Old West was an invention, and the rodeo mirrored that invention. Cowboys were inventions and so were Indians.

Let me give you an example. One summer I was visiting an all-Indian rodeo in White Swan, Washington, trying to get a sense of how the rodeo royalty were selected and what they would do at this local community event held annually on the Yakama Indian Reservation. As the three members of the old court stood up to congratulate the new queen and her princesses, one of the women turned to the others and said laughingly, "It's time to play Indian," and she then proceeded to watch approvingly as the beaded tiara came to rest on a friend's head. They were all dressed in their best Western wear and had slim pressed jeans pulled military-style down over crisp, almost crackly, cowboy boots. Indian cowboys were as natural and artificial to them as Indian fry bread. They played their part with a good amount of laughter washed over the top. It was not only the "cowboy" who was invented; it was also the "Indian."

When I watched the rodeo parade in Omak, I was struck by the limited number of roles the rodeo had for people to play. The rodeo queens rode by with their usual smiles and waves, all sequined and glittered. Several had flashy red-white-and-blue outfits of buckskin and beads. Two local Indians performed hoop dances. A local sheriff posse was dressed up like cowboys, and various Chamber of Commerce people obliged with Western wear.

The rodeo parade was neatly coded into tons of white cowboys and cowgirls and a few red Indians, but the crowd told a different story. To my right sat a group of seven people from a local tribe. A Mexican-American family of four with the father dressed in his Western best strolled up and down the sidewalk. To my left sat an overweight white woman and her seven-year-old son, who clutched a bright purple plastic car. A Chinese-American man leaned in a doorway behind me. We stared at the parade going past.

Larry McMurtry refers to these Old West rituals as games of ghosts, haunted houses mixing nostalgia and the ridiculous. That West has gone, he says. But I disagree. Ghosts usually came back to avenge a past wrong or to warn the living. They trespass on our normal lives, upsetting our sense of reality. Where McMurtry sees ghosts, I see pantomimes, the performers mechanically gesturing to the crowd about a West that never was.

McMurtry also reminds us that lies about the West are often more powerful than the truth. And in that I agree. I have certainly come to understand during this project that hardly anyone likes the truth, especially the truths of history.

I sat on the yellowing grass next to the Pepsi stand, trying to find some shade away from the August heat. Hard-driving country music blasted from the speakers around the fairgrounds, hyping up the crowd that filtered into the stands. I thought about staying where I was and listening to the rodeo from outside the gates. I wanted to let the music float over me as I stretched out and watched the kids play. I did not want to go inside again.

I finally stood up, walked inside the rodeo grounds, and found my seat, close to the chutes. From a distance, I could see the rodeo queens lining up to charge into the arena and wave one more time. I thought about how at her worst the rodeo queen was like a jack-in-the-box who burst out of her container ready and willing to repeat the tired script of pioneer conquest. A ventriloquist of white nationalism, she mimed the hard-hitting action of a make-believe West and then disappeared in a flash. With a snap, the box closed.

Throbbing music shattered the wandering of my mind. The rodeo queens shot out of the side gate at full speed, their arms pumping. Two women almost collided, their horses spinning off, dirt clods hitting the fences. A narrow miss, they regrouped and galloped back toward the gate, horses skidding and sliding as they charged faster, faster than most of the women wanted to go. Once outside the arena gate, they sat back hard on their saddles to regain control. Rodeo queens at the edge. The crowd went wild.

From where I was sitting, I could see the flasks of whiskey the chute guys kept hidden in their pockets. I could smell the shit and urine of the horses and bulls. The sun was merciless. I could barely stand the heat. My neighbors had brought umbrellas to protect then against the 95 degrees, bouncing off aluminum and white lumber. I got up and headed down the steep steps, telling myself it was the heat, but knowing it was my last rodeo.

Driving home, I took a back road through the Colville Indian Reservation. I thought hard about my childhood fascination with the rural West. When I started this book, I was no newcomer to rodeo, though I had never before paid much attention to rodeo queens. In the 1950s, when I was old enough to perch on a fence in western Colorado and watch a ranch rodeo, I was amazed to see a man tossed like a limp rag from his saddle. An eight-year-old, I wondered then, as I do now, whether this contest was make-believe, like the cartoons I gobbled up on television, or whether I could walk back later in the evening to the rickety corral and find the man and his horse sitting down drinking A&W root beer together and laughing about the greenhorns who slurped the act up like chocolate pudding.

As a city child used to the tired streets of Chicago, I was breathless with the crashing of hooves and the sheer bulk of these rodeo cowboys. Westerns pounded across my young mind. I even went to sleep praying for a cowboy to find me and change my life completely. I wanted to make the cold mountain air and endless skies mine, the smell of saddles, the sound of horses, and the red earth of Colorado reachable on my one-speed bicycle. I wanted nothing more than to escape dreary brick tenements near Milwaukee Avenue. I was a city girl enraptured by the power of the American West.

The West was tied to the sensuous knot of my childhood. Each summer, my family visited my uncle in Pueblo, Colorado. He had abandoned the old Polish neighborhood of Chicago for a new start away from the crowded, angry ways of the city. My first pair of cowboy boots was a gift from him when I was six years old. He had driven his pink Lincoln Continental down to Texas and loaded up on Western wear for his nieces and nephews.

It was from Uncle Steve that I first heard the expression "Western justice," and later winced at its meaning. He had left the hard knocks of the river wards in Chicago where Mayor Daley's machine meted out jobs for votes, holding the loyalty of most white immigrant communities. Within a few years, he had become a conservative Colorado Republican who talked about "stringing" up criminals.

He became particularly fond of palomino horses and before he died was part-owner of a ranch in Wolf Creek Pass, Colorado. He had six-shooters, collected cowboy hats, and practically slept in his boots. Adamantly anti-Communist, he stayed close to his Catholic roots but found a flamboyant form of expression in the guise of a Western man. My uncle talked the cowboy talk and walked the cowboy walk. Frankly, I found it amazing. Since then, I have never doubted the power of self-transformation and the strange hold the rural West has on Americans.

I dropped down to the Columbia River and tried to imagine this land without the dams, without the power plants, without the rodeo. For miles, monster metal trellises strode across the hills, carrying power lines needed to run my CD player and hair dryer. I glanced in the rearview mirror and saw the beginning of a roasted-red sunset, and I tried to think about the worlds lost under the river's flow.

How can the story of the American West return to its peoples both the history and beauty of its landscape? Can the West produce a cultural ritual, connected to borders and the politics of place, that can move and engage communities without the booster-ism of patriotic pride? Would it be willing to listen to neighbors who live on reservations, work in the apple orchards, or pump gas? Is it possible to move the tale away from a monolithic telling, droning on and on like a dream machine, silencing all critical thought? The stultifying cost of this national myth of the West is precisely the loss of people and place. I thought again about the revised Happy Canyon pageant at the Pendleton Round-up. The Indian sections stressed tragedy and loss, the cowboy sections were loaded with slapstick and Wild West shoot-'em-up scenes. The whole fell apart into a series of incoherent and schizophrenic tableaus of Western clichés. The attempts to represent history floundered against the need to keep the crowd laughing. In the closing scenes, all the discordant notes were wrapped in the American flag.

I took the slow way home, letting the tape recorder of my mind wind down, glancing out the car window into the evening light that made farmhouses into glowing white light boxes. The golden sheen of the wheat fields created a surreal landscape. Scattered horses stood out against a steel-blue sky. After four hours of driving through small towns with sagging main streets, I was finally close to home.

I passed through a bombed-out shell of a town, struggling to rebuild a cluster of stores. There was no gas station here, no golden arches, no Wal-Mart greeters. A small girl with a cowgirl hat on a bright red bike stared at me as I slowed down to stop at the only crossroads in town. She twisted her bike around and headed off at full speed toward the patch of green called a park.

I waved at her back and headed home, sobered at the way the rural West was reduced to pasteboard cutouts for mass consumption and convinced of the need for the human imagination to face the deep, swift currents of our lives in this land.

Acknowledgments

This book had a life of its own and I merely followed. One person led me to another; one story could not be told without the next. First, I want to thank the women who let me into their kitchens, living rooms, and barns and decided that the years they had been rodeo royalty might indeed add to our understanding of who we are as Americans. To provide these women with some privacy, I have used only their first names or have changed their names throughout.

In following these stories, I also had to go down the rodeo road and talk with rodeo board members and people who volunteered on royalty com mittees as chaperones, promoters, dress designers, and public relations consultants. They let me see what was involved in running a rodeo from the community perspective. On the national level, I had the benefit of speaking with and listening to speeches of corporate sponsors and professional rodeo organizers.

In the early stages of this project, I was fortunate to receive a summer fellowship from the Charles Redd Center for Western Studies at Brigham Young University. This initial funding not only got me started with gasoline money, audiotapes, and time but also gave me the inkling that someone might want to listen to these conversations. Continued work on this book has been greatly assisted by two other sources. As the Edward R. Meyer Professor of English and American Studies and later the Lewis E. and Stella

G. Buchanan Professor of English at Washington State University, I was given research funds to sustain and finish this project. Also, when I was on sabbatical leave in Hong Kong, the David C. Lam Institute for East-West Studies at Hong Kong Baptist University graciously provided me with an office, a computer, and staff support to work on the writing of this manuscript. I presented a section of this book at the Lam Institute and benefited from hearing reactions about the cultural ritual of the rodeo from outside the perspective of the United States. An international audience is the best place to render visible the peculiar shape of national storytelling.

Sections of Chapter 6 appeared as a photo essay in *Frontiers: A Journal of Women Studies*, vol. 17, no. 3, 1996. I would like to give special thanks to Susan Armitage and Teresa Jordan for talking with me about this project and encouraging me to go forward with this work. I hope the end result has not strayed too far from the original idea.

A book finally comes into being with the help of readers, friends, and fellow writers. I want to thank Dee Tomson and Betty Tukey for helping me understand the world of horses. I want to thank my sisters, Lenore Elsener and Monica Munaretto, and my brothers, Stephen and Joseph Burbick, and their families for their constant support. Ann McCormack, Bobbie Conner, Sandi Lee, Darlene Turner, Judy Bothum, Jenine Williamson, Janie Tippett, Jack Sweek, and Dave Hamley provided valuable background information. The Lewiston Roundup Association, the *Lewiston Morning Tribune*, and Matt Johnson at Howdyshell Photos helped immensely with visual images. Ran Huntsberry, Gerry Young, and Dorene Magera never gave up on the writing. My daughter, Claire Huntsberry, my agent, Sandra Dijkstra, and my tough but wise editor, Kate Darnton, played essential roles. Finally, this book would not have been possible without my husband, Alex Kuo, who read and reread each page, following syntax and sense to help me understand what the words say.

Works Consulted

Western History

Adams, Andy. *The Log of a Cowboy: A Narrative of Old Trail Days*.
Lincoln: University of Nebraska Press, 1964.

Allen, Margaret Day. *Lewiston Country: An Armchair History*. Lewiston,
ID: Nez Perce County Historical Society, 1990.

Allmendinger, Blake. *The Cowboy: Representations of Labor in an
American Work Culture*. New York: Oxford University Press, 1992.

Armitage, Susan, and Elizabeth Jameson, eds. *The Women's West*. Norman:
University of Oklahoma Press, 1987.

Blew, Mary Clearman. *All but the Waltz: A Memoir of Five Generations in
the Life of a Montana Family*. New York: Penguin Books, 1991.

Dana, Richard Henry, Jr. *Two Years Before the Mast*. New York: Signet,
1964.

Douglas, William O. *Of Men and Mountains*. San Francisco: Chronicle
Books, 1990.

Farley, Ronnie. *Cowgirls: Contemporary Portraits of the American West*.
New York: Crown Trade Paperbacks, 1995.

Hickey, Dave. "A Dialectical Inquiry into the Recurring Fantasy of the
Equestrian Herdsman (Singing Variety)." In Lonn Taylor and Ingrid
Maar, eds., *The American Cowboy*. New York: Harper and Row,
Publishers, 1983.

Jameson, Elizabeth, and Susan Armitage, eds. *Writing the Range: Race, Class, and Culture in the Women's West*. Norman: University of Oklahoma Press, 1997.

Jordan, Teresa. *Cowgirls: Women of the American West*. Lincoln: University of Nebraska Press, 1992.

————. *Riding the White Horse Home: A Western Family Album*. New York: Vintage, 1993.

Jordan, Terry G. *North American Cattle-Ranching Frontiers: Origins, Diffusion, and Differentiation*. Albuquerque: University of New Mexico Press, 1993.

Limerick, Patricia Nelson. *The Legacy of Conquest: The Unbroken Past of the American West*. New York: W. W. Norton and Co., 1987.

MacKinnon, Janice R., and Stephen R. MacKinnon. *Agnes Smedley: The Life and Times of an American Radical*. Berkeley: University of California Press, 1988.

McMurtry, Larry. "Westward Ho Hum: What the New Historians Have Done to the Old West." *New Republic* 22 (October 1990): 32–38.

Milner, Clyde A., Carol A. O'Connor, and Martha A. Sandweiss. *The Oxford History of the American West*. New York: Oxford University Press, 1994.

Morrissey, Katherine G. *Mental Territories: Mapping the Inland Empire*. Ithaca: Cornell University Press, 1997.

Roe, JoAnn. *Frank Matsura: Frontier Photographer*. Seattle: Madrona Publishers, 1981.

Sandoz, Mari. *Old Jules*. Lincoln: University of Nebraska Press, 1985.

Schwantes, Carlos A. *The Pacific Northwest: An Interpretive History*. Lincoln: University of Nebraska Press, 1989.

Slatta, Richard W. *Cowboys of the Americas*. New Haven: Yale University Press, 1990.

Slotkin, Richard. *Gunfighter Nation: The Myth of the Frontier in Twentieth-Century America*. New York: Atheneum, 1992.

Smedley, Agnes. *Daughter of Earth*. 1929. Reprint, New York: Feminist Press, 1986.

Starrs, Paul F. *Let the Cowboy Ride: Cattle Ranching in the American West.* Baltimore: Johns Hopkins University Press, 1998.

Weston, Jack. *The Real American Cowboy.* New York: Schocken Books, 1985.

White, Richard. *"It's Your Misfortune and None of My Own": A New History of the American West.* Norman: University of Oklahoma Press, 1991.

Worster, Donald. *Rivers of Empire: Water, Aridity, and the Growth of the American West.* New York: Pantheon Books, 1985.

_____. *Under Western Skies: Nature and History in the American West.* New York: Oxford University Press, 1992.

Rodeo History

Allen, Michael. *Rodeo Cowboys in the North American Imagination.* Reno: University of Nevada Press, 1998.

Annerino, John. *Roughstock: The Toughest Events in Rodeo.* New York: Four Walls Eight Windows, 2000.

Bergner, Daniel. *God of the Rodeo: The Quest for Redemption in Louisiana's Angola Prison.* New York: Ballantine Books, 1998.

Blackstone, Sarah J. *Buckskins, Bullets, and Business: A History of Buffalo Bill's Wild West.* New York: Greenwood Press, 1986.

Eisner, Lisa. *Rodeo Girl.* Los Angeles: Greybull Press, 2000.

Fredriksson, Kristine. *American Rodeo: From Buffalo Bill to Big Business.* College Station: Texas A&M University Press, 1985.

Gray, James H. *A Brand of Its Own: The 100 Year History of the Calgary Exhibition and Stampede.* Saskatoon, Saskatchewan: Western Producer Prairie Books, 1985.

Hendra, Tony. "Man and Bull: Afternoons of a Young Torero." *Harper's* (November 1996): 69–77.

Iverson, Peter. *Riders of the West: Portraits from Indian Rodeo.* Seattle: University of Washington Press, 1999.

Kerouac, Jack. *On the Road.* New York: Penguin, 1957.

Kesey, Ken, with Ken Babbs. *Last Go Round: A Real Western*. New York: Penguin, 1994.

Lawrence, Elizabeth Atwood. *Hoofbeats and Society: Studies of Human-Horse Interactions*. Bloomington: Indiana University Press, 1985.

———. *Rodeo: An Anthropologist Looks at the Wild and the Tame*. Knoxville: University of Tennessee Press, 1982.

LeCompte, Mary Lou. *Cowgirls of the Rodeo: Pioneer Professional Athletes*. Chicago: University of Illinois Press, 1993.

McFadden, Cyra. *Rain or Shine: A Family Memoir*. New York: Alfred A. Knopf, 1986.

Moses, L. G., *Wild West Shows and the Images of American Indians, 1883–1933*. Albuquerque: University of New Mexico Press, 1996.

Reddin, Paul. *Wild West Shows*. Urbana: University of Illinois Press, 1999.

Rupp, Virgil. *Let 'Er Buck: A History of the Pendleton Round-Up*. Pendleton, OR: Master Printers, 1985.

Russell, Don. *The Wild West: A History of Wild West Shows*. Fort Worth, TX: Amon Carter Museum of Western Art, 1970.

Serpa, Louise L. *Rodeo*. Notes by Larry McMurtry. New York: Aperture, 1994.

Stoeltje, Beverly J. "Gender Representations in Performance: The Cowgirl and the Hostess." *Journal of Folklore Research* 25 (3) (September–December 1988): 219–241.

———. "Power and the Ritual Genres: American Rodeo." *Western Folklore* 52 (April 1993): 135–156.

Taylor, Allan. "As Bull Riding's Popularity Grows, So Do Injuries." *Palouse Living* 25 (36), September 22, 1998, 1.

Westermeier, Clifford P. *Man, Beast, Dust: The Story of Rodeo*. Lincoln: University of Nebraska Press, 1947.

Wooden, Wayne S., and Gavin Ehringer. *Rodeo in America: Wranglers, Roughstock, and Paydirt*. Lawrence: University Press of Kansas, 1996.

Zarzyski, Paul. "Hooked on Rodeo." *Montana Magazine*, September–October 1985, 12–16.

Western Popular Culture

Avedon, Richard. *In the American West*. New York: Harry N. Abrams, 1985.

Bold, Christine. *Selling the Wild West: Popular Western Fiction, 1860–1960*. Bloomington: Indiana University Press, 1987.

Borland, Hal. *When the Legends Die*. New York: Bantam, 1963.

Burg, David F. *Chicago's White City of 1893*. Lexington: University Press of Kentucky, 1976.

Buscombe, Edward, ed. *The BFI Companion to the Western*. New York: Atheneum, 1988.

Evans, Nicholas. *The Horse Whisperer*. New York: Dell, 1995.

Havinghurst, Walter. *Annie Oakley of the Wild West*. Lincoln: University of Nebraska Press, 1992.

MacDonald, J. Fred. *Who Shot the Sheriff? The Rise and Fall of the Television Western*. New York: Praeger, 1987.

Mitchell, Lee Clark. *Westerns: Making the Man in Fiction and Film*. Chicago: University of Chicago Press, 1996.

Tichi, Cecelia. *High Lonesome: The American Culture of Country Music*. Chapel Hill: University of North Carolina Press, 1994.

Tompkins, Jane. *West of Everything: The Inner Life of Westerns*. New York: Oxford University Press, 1992.

Wister, Owen. *The Virginian: A Horseman of the Plains*. New York: Viking Penguin, 1988.

Native American History and Culture

Axtell, Horace, and Margo Aragon. *A Little Bit of Wisdom: Conversations with a Nez Perce Elder*. Lewiston, ID: Confluence Press, 1997.

Berkhofer, Robert F. *The White Man's Indian: The History of an Idea from Columbus to the Present*. New York: Knopf, 1978.

Bird, S. Elizabeth, ed. *Dressing in Feathers: The Construction of the Indian in American Popular Culture*. Boulder: Westview Press, 1996.

Deloria, Philip J. *Playing Indian*. New Haven: Yale University Press, 1998.

Dove, Mourning (Hum-Ishu-Ma). *Cogewea: The Half-Blood*. Lincoln: University of Nebraska Press, 1981.

Evans, Steven Ross. *Voice of the Old Wolf: Lucullus Virgil McWhorter and the Nez Perce Indians*. Pullman: Washington State University Press, 1996.

Fletcher, Alice C. *Indian Games and Dance with Native Song*. 1915. Reprint, Lincoln: University of Nebraska, 1994.

Gay, E. Jane. *With the Nez Perces: Alice Fletcher in the Field, 1889–92*. Lincoln: University of Nebraska Press, 1981.

Gifford, Barry, ed. *Selected Writings of Edward S. Curtis*. Berkeley: Creative Arts Book Company, 1976.

Graybill, Florence Curtis, and Victor Boesen. *Edward Sheriff Curtis: Visions of a Vanishing Race*. Boston: Houghton Company, 1976.

Heth, Charlotte, gen. ed. *Native American Dance: Ceremonies and Social Traditions*. Washington, DC: Smithsonian Institution and the National Museum of the American Indian, 1993.

Hunn, Eugene S. *Nch'i-Wána "The Big River": Mid-Columbia Indians and Their Land*. Seattle: University of Washington, 1990.

James, Caroline. *Nez Perce Women in Transition, 1877–1990*. Moscow: University of Idaho Press, 1996.

Jones, Patti. "Wisdom for the 21st Century." *Moscow Pullman Daily News,* June 12, 1997.

Josephy, Alvin M., Jr. *The Nez Perce Indians and the Opening of the Northwest*. New York: Houghton Mifflin, 1997.

Kilpatrick, Jacquelyn. *Celluloid Indians: Native Americans and Film*. Lincoln: University of Nebraska Press, 1999.

Klein, Laura F., and Lillian A. Ackerman. *Women and Power in Native North America*. Norman: University of Oklahoma Press, 1995.

Laubin, Reginald, and Gladys Laubin. *Indian Dances of North America: Their Importance to Indian Life*. Norman: University of Oklahoma Press, 1977.

Mark, Joan. *A Stranger in Her Native Land: Alice Fletcher and the American Indians*. Lincoln: University of Nebraska Press, 1988.

Marra, Ben. *Powwow: Images Along the Red Road.* New York: Harry N. Abrams, 1996.

Maud, Ralph. *A Guide to B.C. Indian Myth and Legend.* Vancouver, B.C.: Talonbooks, 1982.

McBeth, Kate. *The Nez Perces Since Lewis and Clark.* Moscow: University of Idaho Press, 1993.

McWhorter, Lucullus Virgil. *Yellow Wolf: His Own Story.* Caldwell, ID: Caxton Printers, 1995.

Miller, Jay, ed. *Mourning Dove: A Salishan Autobiography.* Lincoln: University of Nebraska Press, 1990.

Momaday, N. Scott. *House Made of Dawn.* New York: Harper and Row, 1968.

Phinney, Archie. *Nez Percé Texts.* New York: Columbia University Press, 1934.

Relander, Click. *Drummers and Dreamers.* Seattle: Caxton Printers, 1986.

Rice, David G. *Marmes Rockshelter Archaeological Site: Southern Columbia Plateau.* Pullman: Washington State University Laboratory of Anthropology, 1969.

Roalf, Peggy, ed. *Strong Hearts: Native American Visions and Voices.* New York: Aperture, 1995.

Rountree, Helen C. *Pocahontas's People: The Powhatan Indians of Virginia Through Four Centuries.* Norman: University of Oklahoma Press, 1990.

Ruby, Robert H., and John A. Brown. *Dreamer-Prophets of the Columbia Plateau: Smohalla and Skolaskin.* Norman: University of Oklahoma Press, 1989.

_____. *Half-Sun on the Columbia: A Biography of Chief Moses.* Norman: University of Oklahoma Press, 1965.

Scholder, Fritz. *Indian Kitsch: The Use and Misuse of Indian Images.* Flagstaff, AZ: Northland Press, 1979.

Trafzer, Clifford E., and Richard D. Scheuerman. *Renegade Tribe: The Palouse Indians and the Invasion of the Inland Pacific Northwest.* Pullman: Washington State University Press, 1986.

Utley, Robert M. *The Indian Frontier of the American West, 1846–1890.* Albuquerque: University of New Mexico Press, 1984.

Vestal, Stanley. *Sitting Bull: Champion of the Sioux*. Norman: University of Oklahoma Press, 1957.

Walker, Deward E., Jr. *Conflict and Schism in Nez Perce Acculturation: A Study of Religion and Politics*. Moscow: University of Idaho Press, 1985.

Willard, Helen. *Pow-Wow and Other Yakima Indian Traditions*. Prosser, WA: Roza Run Publishing, 1990.

Feminist Criticism and Theory

Adams, Carol J., and Josephine Donovan, eds. *Animals and Women: Feminist Theoretical Explorations*. Durham, NC: Duke University Press, 1995.

Behar, Ruth, and Deborah A. Gordon. *Women Writing Culture*. Berkeley: University of California Press, 1995.

Butler, Judith. *Gender Trouble: Feminism and the Subversion of Identity*. New York: Routledge, 1990.

Butler, Judith, and Joan W. Scott. *Feminists Theorize the Political*. New York: Routledge, 1992.

Cohen, Colleen Ballerino, Richard Wilk, and Beverly Stoeltje. *Beauty Queens on the Global Stage: Gender, Contests, and Power*. New York: Routledge, 1996.

Donaldson, Laura E. *Decolonizing Feminisms: Race, Gender, and Empire-Building*. Chapel Hill: University of North Carolina Press, 1992.

Frankenberg, Ruth. *White Women, Race Matters: The Social Construction of Whiteness*. Minneapolis: University of Minnesota Press, 1993.

Friedan, Betty. *The Feminine Mystique*. New York: Norton, 1963.

Jayawardena, Kumari. *The White Woman's Other Burden: Western Women and South Asia During British Rule*. London: Routledge, 1995.

McClintock, Anne. *Imperial Leather: Race, Gender, and Sexuality in the Colonial Contest*. New York: Routledge, 1995.

Radway, Janice. *Reading the Romance: Women, Patriarchy, and Popular Literature*. Chapel Hill: University of North Carolina Press, 1984.

Visweswaran, Kamala. *Fictions of Feminist Ethnography*. Minneapolis: University of Minnesota Press, 1994.

Wolf, Naomi. *The Beauty Myth: How Images of Beauty Are Used Against Women*. New York: Doubleday, 1991.

Theories of Nationalism

Anderson, Benedict. *Imagined Communities: Reflections on the Origin and Spread of Nationalism*. 2nd ed. London: Verso, 1991.

Berlant, Lauren. *The Anatomy of National Fantasy: Hawthorne, Utopia, and Everyday Life*. Chicago: University of Chicago Press, 1991.

Eley, Geoff, and Ronald Grigor Suny. *Becoming National*. New York: Oxford University Press, 1996.

Hobsbawm, Eric. "Mass-Producing Traditions: Europe, 1870–1914." In Eric Hobsbawm and Terence Ranger, eds., *The Invention of Tradition*. New York: Cambridge University Press, 1983.

_____. *Nations and Nationalism Since 1780: Programme, Myth, Reality*. New York: Cambridge University Press, 1990.

Hutchinson, John, and Anthony D. Smith, eds. *Nationalism*. New York: Oxford University Press, 1994.

Ignatieff, Michael. *Blood and Belonging: Journeys into the New Nationalism*. New York: Penguin, 1993.

Mosse, George L. *Nationalism and Sexuality: Middle-Class Morality and Sexual Norms in Modern Europe*. Madison: University of Wisconsin Press, 1985.

Nationalisms and National Identities. Special issue of *Feminist Review* 44 (Summer 1993).

Parker, Andrew, Mary Russo, Doris Sommer, and Patricia Yaeger, eds. *Nationalisms and Sexualities*. New York: Routledge, 1992.

Pateman, Carole. *The Sexual Contract*. Cambridge: Polity, 1998.

Yuval-Davis, Nira. *Gender and Nation*. London: Sage Publications, 1997.

Cultural Studies

Baudrillard, Jean. *America*. New York: Verso, 1988.

Benjamin, Walter. *Illuminationen*. New York: Harcourt, Brace and World, 1968.

Bourdieu, Pierre. *The Field of Cultural Production*. New York: Columbia University Press, 1993.

Buch-Morss, Susan. *The Dialectics of Seeing: Walter Benjamin and the Arcades Project*. Cambridge: MIT Press, 1989.

Clifford, James, and George E. Marcus. *Writing Culture: The Poetics and Politics of Ethnography*. Berkeley: University of California Press, 1986.

Debord, Guy. *Comments on the Society of the Spectacle*. New York: Verso, 1990.

During, Simon, ed. *The Cultural Studies Reader*. New York: Routledge, 1993.

Dyer, Richard. "White." *Screen* 29 (4) (Autumn 1988): 44–64.

Hebdige, Dick. *Subculture: The Meaning of Style*. New York: Methuen, 1979.

Karp, Ivan, and Steven D. Lavine, eds. *Exhibiting Cultures: The Poetics and Politics of Museum Display*. Washington, DC: Smithsonian Institution Press, 1991.

Limón, José E. *Dancing with the Devil: Society and Cultural Poetics in Mexican-American South Texas*. Madison: University of Wisconsin Press, 1994.

Murkerji, Chandra, and Michael Schudson. *Rethinking Popular Culture: Contemporary Perspectives in Cultural Studies*. Berkeley: University of California Press, 1991.

Stallybrass, Peter, and Allon White. *The Politics and Poetics of Transgression*. London: Methuen, 1986.

Taussig, Michael T. *The Devil and Commodity Fetishism in South America*. Chapel Hill: University of North Carolina Press, 1980.

Turner, Victor. *Dramas, Fields, and Metaphors: Symbolic Action in Human Society*. Ithaca: Cornell University Press, 1974.

Equine History and Culture

Budiansky, Stephen. *The Nature of Horses: Exploring Equine Evolution, Intelligence, and Behavior.* New York: Free Press, 1997.

Dorrance, Tom. *True Unity: Willing Communication Between Horse and Human.* Fresno, CA: Word Dancer Press, 1994.

Roberts, Monty. *The Man Who Listens to Horses.* New York: Random House, 1997.

Shepard, Paul. *The Others: How Animals Made Us Human.* Washington, DC: Island Press, 1996.

Tuan, Yi-Fu. *Dominance and Affection: The Making of Pets.* New Haven: Yale University Press, 1984.

A Note on the Photographs

The photographs in this book depict women I interviewed or are closely related in period and locale.

Queen Betty, 1931: *Underwood Archives*

Joan, Lewiston Roundup, 1949: *Lewiston Morning Tribune (LMT)*

JoAnne, 1945: *Family Photograph*

Lewiston Roundup, 1947: *LMT*

Leah with President Harry S. Truman, Pendleton Round-Up, 1952: *Howdyshell Photos*

Jean, Lewiston Roundup, 1954: *LMT*

Jean, Publicity shot for Lewiston Roundup, 1954: *LMT*

Chief Joseph Days Court, 1953: *LMT*

Susan receiving prize from Bob Barker, Miss Rodeo America, 1959: *LMT*

Miss Rodeo America competition, Flamingo Hotel, Las Vegas, 1959: *LMT*

Lewiston Roundup, 1976: *LMT*

Lewiston Roundup Promotional Shot, Rodeo Court with Slim Pickens, 1960s: *LMT*

Lewiston Roundup Queen, 1990: *LMT*

Pendleton Round-Up Parade, 2001: *Joan Burbick*

Miss Rodeo America contestants for the 1997 Crown: *Joan Burbick*

Index

PublicAffairs is a publishing house founded in 1997. It is a tribute to the standards, values, and flair of three persons who have served as mentors to countless reporters, writers, editors, and book people of all kinds, including me.

I. F. Stone, proprietor of *I. F. Stone's Weekly*, combined a commitment to the First Amendment with entrepreneurial zeal and reporting skill and became one of the great independent journalists in American history. At the age of eighty, Izzy published *The Trial of Socrates*, which was a national bestseller. He wrote the book after he taught himself ancient Greek.

Benjamin C. Bradlee was for nearly thirty years the charismatic editorial leader of *The Washington Post*. It was Ben who gave the *Post* the range and courage to pursue such historic issues as Watergate. He supported his reporters with a tenacity that made them fearless, and it is no accident that so many became authors of influential, best-selling books.

Robert L. Bernstein, the chief executive of Random House for more than a quarter century, guided one of the nation's premier publishing houses. Bob was personally responsible for many books of political dissent and argument that challenged tyranny around the globe. He is also the founder and was the longtime chair of Human Rights Watch, one of the most respected human rights organizations in the world.

.　　.　　.

For fifty years, the banner of Public Affairs Press was carried by its owner, Morris B. Schnapper, who published Gandhi, Nasser, Toynbee, Truman, and about 1,500 other authors. In 1983 Schnapper was described by *The Washington Post* as "a redoubtable gadfly." His legacy will endure in the books to come.

Peter Osnos, *Publisher*